STUDY GUIDE

Prepared by Teresa Vanderweide
Mount Royal College

CONTEMPORARY LINGUISTIC ANALYSIS
An Introduction

Fifth Edition

William O'Grady
University of Hawaii

John Archibald
University of Calgary

PEARSON
Longman

Toronto

ISBN 0-321-24302-1

Executive Editor: Christine Cozens
Senior Developmental Editor: Lise Dupont
Production Editor: Avivah Wargon
Production Manager: Wendy Moran

7 8 9 DPC 08 07 06

Printed and bound in Canada.

CONTENTS

PREFACE

This workbook is intended to accompany the fifth edition of *Contemporary Linguistic Analysis: An Introduction*. It originally began as a series of worksheets distributed to students in class and gradually expanded to include brief explanations of text material and practice exercises, as well as review sheets. All of the material that came to be included in the workbook was either modified or designed to supplement the content in *Contemporary Linguistic Analysis*, the text being used for introductory linguistics. As the workbook evolved, it became more generic and, as a result, potentially useful to virtually any instructor of introductory linguistics using *Contemporary Linguistic Analysis*.

The workbook contains a preview of major concepts followed by six chapters that correspond to the core components of linguistics: phonetics, phonology, morphology, syntax, and semantics, as well as historical linguistics. These are the main areas in which students typically require a great deal of exposure to, and practice with, the methods of analysis used in that particular branch of linguistics. It is hoped that this workbook will help fulfill this need. Each chapter in the workbook begins with a list of the main topics and/or concepts found within. It then contains explanations of these important concepts followed by practice exercises. All chapters include reminders of important concepts that students need to be familiar with, and conclude with a review list intended as a study guide. Throughout the workbook, the focus is always on the content of the corresponding *Contemporary Linguistic Analysis* chapter. Finally, while every attempt was made to include as much language data as possible, the workbook does tend to emphasize Canadian English, the starting point for most students as they learn and become familiar with the methodology used in linguistic analysis.

I gratefully acknowledge contributions made by Carrie Dyck, Elaine Sorensen, Leone Sveinson, Joyce Hildebrand, and Lorna Rowsell, without whom this workbook would not have been possible. I would like to thank all the reviewers for their comments, especially Carrie Dyck and William O'Grady for their invaluable suggestions and advice, which have improved the overall quality of the workbook. Thanks also go to Elizabeth Ritter for using a version of the workbook with her students and providing valuable feedback. Finally, I extend my sincere thanks and gratitude to Michael Dobrovolsky for his continued inspiration, support, and encouragement.

For Chris

CHAPTER 1. LANGUAGE: A PREVIEW

The following are some of the important concepts found in this chapter. Make sure you are familiar with them!

1. Specialization
2. Creativity
3. Linguistic Competence
4. Grammar

SPECIALIZATION

Humans are specialized for language. The characteristics below illustrate some of the aspects of our special capacity for language.

1. Speech Organs

Our lungs, vocal cords, tongue, teeth, lips, and nasal passages are used for breathing and eating, and for producing the sounds of our language.

2. Speech Breathing

We have the ability to breathe not only for survival but also for speech. Speech breathing uses a different set of muscles and different lung pressure and exhalation time than our normal breathing!

3. Speech Perception

We are also equipped for speech perception, and we have the ability at birth. Studies have shown that newborns are able to perceive subtle differences between sounds and are even able to perceive sounds they have never heard before.

4. Specialized Brain Areas

The human brain is structured for language. Our brains appear to have specialized areas dedicated to language production and comprehension—areas that are not found in other species.

This specialization for language sets us apart from all other creatures!

CREATIVITY

Human language is creative. That is, language does not provide us with a set of pre-packaged messages. Rather, it allows us to produce and understand new words and sentences whenever needed. However, there are limitations on both the form and interpretation of new words and sentences. Linguists attempt to identify and understand these limitations.

Exercise!   Arrange the words "bird", "worm", "catches", "early", "every", "the", and "a" into an English sentence.

Think of other arrangements of the same words that result in different sentences from the one you just put together.

Think about how you could arrange the words so that the sentence you create is not an acceptable English sentence.

LINGUISTIC COMPETENCE

Linguistic Competence can be defined as subconscious knowledge which enables the native speakers of a language to produce and understand an unlimited number of both familiar and novel utterances. The native speakers of a language are those who have acquired it as children in a home rather than in a classroom.

Linguists divide the subconscious knowledge that the native speakers of a language share into the following fields of study:

1. Phonetics: the study of the articulation and perception of speech sounds

2. Phonology: the study of how speech sounds pattern in language

3. Morphology: the study of word structure and word formation

4. Syntax: the study of sentence structure

5. Semantics: the study of the meaning of words and sentences

This subconscious knowledge allows the speakers of a language to produce an infinite number of sentences, many of which we have never uttered or heard before. We don't memorize language: we create it.

Exercise! Your linguistic competence allows you to decide whether new words and novel sentences are acceptable or not. Test your linguistic competence by answering the following questions.

1. Put a check mark beside those words that are possible English words.

   a. tlim _____   e. plog _____

   b. stuken _____   f. skpit _____

   c. tseg _____   g. ngan _____

   d. fomp _____   h. breb _____

   Think about why some of the above are not possible English words. (HINT: Look at the combination of sounds found at the beginning of the words.)

2. Put a check mark beside those words that are possible English words.

   a. speakless _____   d. reglorify_____

   b. beautifulness _____   e. horseable _____

   c. unrug _____   f. weedic _____

   Think about why some of the above are not possible English words. (HINT: Think about the prefix or suffix and its contribution to the meaning of the word.)

3. Put a check mark beside those sentences that are possible English sentences.

a. The building is swept yesterday evening.   _____

b. The building is swept every morning.   _____

c. Every child should obey his parents.   _____

d. Somebody left their gloves in the theatre.   _____

e. George surprised Mary with a party.   _____

f. Joe surprised the stone.   _____

Think about why some of the above are not possible English sentences.

GRAMMAR

Grammar, to a linguist, refers to all the elements of our linguistic competence: phonetics, phonology, morphology, syntax, and semantics. In very general terms, grammar can be defined as the mental system of knowledge needed to form and interpret the sounds, words, and sentences of our language. The study of grammar is central to understanding language and what it means to know a language. This is because all languages have sounds, words and sentences; all grammars allow for the expression of any thought; all grammars share common principles and tendencies called universals; and all grammars change over time. However, our grammatical knowledge is subconscious: we can decide what sounds right and what does not even though we may not be sure about why this is so.

There are two perspectives on grammar: prescriptive and descriptive. A prescriptive grammar gives the socially accepted rules within a language, while a descriptive grammar is an objective description of the knowledge that native speakers share. Examine the boxes below (adapted from *The Verbal Edge*, Readers Digest, 1994) and see if you can tell which type of grammar is being exemplified.

WRONG: "Between you and I …
RIGHT: "Between you and me …

On an episode of the TV sitcom "Home Improvement", handyman Tim Taylor said of competitor Bob Vila, "A lot of people think there's a big rivalry between Bob and I."

That may sound correct, but the pronoun *I* is wrong here. *Between* is a preposition, and prepositions are always followed by objects. *I* is a subject or nominative pronoun. So are *he, she, we,* and *they*. Objective pronouns that follow a preposition are *me, you, him, her, us,* and *them*.

Use the rhyme "Between thee and me" as a reminder.

WRONG: "She is older than me."
RIGHT: "She is older than I."

Unlike *between*, the word *than* is not a preposition; it's a conjunction—a word that joins two sentence, words, or phrases. In this case there are two sentences: (1) "She is older" and (2) "I am"—but the *am* has been dropped, and that throws people off.

In a comparison joined by *than* or *as*, just complete the sentence, and the correct word will be obvious. You wouldn't say "He is smarter than me am", so it must be "He is smarter than I".

WRONG: "Who do I ask?"
RIGHT: "Whom do I ask?"

Who and *whom* will never stump you if you remember: *Who* is generally appropriate whenever you use *he, she,* or *they*; *whom* acts as a substitute for *him, her,* or *them*. Sometimes it helps to recast a question into a statement. In this example, you'd never say "I ask he", so the correct wording is "Whom do I ask?" ("But that sounds stuffy", you say. Yes—which is why the incorrect "Who do I ask?" is sometimes used in informal situations.

WRONG: "The demand for durable goods such as cars and home appliances were unchanged last month."
RIGHT: "The demand for durable goods such as cars and home appliances was unchanged last month."

A CNN news anchor delivered this blooper, which goes to show that even professionals err. The mistake was mating a plural verb with a singular subject. And it often happens as it did here: The subject of the sentence, *demand*, was singular, but it got separated from the verb by the plural phrase *such as cars and home appliances*. Distracted by these particulars, the anchor forgot that she was speaking in the singular and used a plural verb. Keep your mind on the subject—what it is you're talking about.

The above are all examples of a prescriptivist view on language. While a prescriptivist grammar is useful in helping people learn a foreign language, in that it contains the socially accepted rules for language use, linguists are more interested in descriptive grammar.

Spot the Difference!   Each of the following aspects of linguistic competence contains two statements. See if you can identify which statement is prescriptivist and which is descriptivist. Do this by writing either D.G. (Descriptive Grammar) or P.G. (Prescriptive Grammar) beside each statement.

1. Sounds

_____ The English words **Mary, merry**, and **marry** should be pronounced differently because they are spelled differently.

_____ English contains over twenty different consonant sounds.

Think about how many different vowel sounds are found in English.

Do all languages have the same consonant and/or vowel sounds? Think of a language that has different vowel or consonant sounds from English.

2. Words

_____ The use of **thunk** and not **thought** as the past tense of the verb **think** is an example of how change is causing the English language to deteriorate.

_____ Many nouns in English are formed by adding the suffix **ment** to words (e.g., achievement, government, judgement).

Think about why no English speaker would construct the word **chairment**.

3. Sentences

_____ There are at least two ways in English to make a sentence refer to the future.

_____ The auxiliary **will** should be used with the 3rd person singular (i.e., *he, she, it*), whereas **shall** should be used for all other persons (e.g., He will go, but we shall stay.).

Think of two different ways to change the sentence ***The horses eat hay.*** to refer to the future.

Think about how other languages make statements refer to future time.

4. Meaning

    _____   The word ***cool*** should only be used to refer to temperature.

    _____   Many words in a language often have opposite meanings (e.g., hot/cold, light/dark).

Think about how the meaning of a sentence is different from the meaning of the words that comprise it.

QUICK REMINDER!

Linguistics is the study of the structure of human language, and linguists attempt to describe, in an objective and non-judgmental fashion, the internalized and unconscious knowledge which the native speakers of a language share, and which allows them to both speak and understand their language. While the primary focus of this guide is on English, many of the principles and theories discussed apply to all other languages as well.

REVIEW EXERCISE

Each of the statements below illustrates a concept found in Chapter One. For each statement, determine which concept is being illustrated. Do this by writing the number of the concept beside each statement. The first is done for you.

Concepts:
1. Linguistic Competence
2. Prescriptive Grammar
3. Descriptive Grammar
4. Universal (i.e., something common to all languages)

Statements:

_____4_____ All languages have a way of making negatives.

_____ Speakers of Canadian English know that one way to make questions is to move an auxiliary verb ahead of the subject noun phrase.

_____ Many nouns in English are formed by adding -ness to an adjective; for example: sadness, silliness, and happiness.

_____ 'brung' should never be used as the past tense of 'bring'.

_____ Every language has a set of vowels and consonants.

_____ Speakers of any language are capable of producing an unlimited number of novel sentences.

_____ In English, there is no theoretical limit on the number of adjectives that can occur before a noun.

_____ In the sentence "My friend is smarter than me", 'me' is incorrect because it is an object pronoun and this comparative construction requires the subject pronoun 'I'.

_____ In English, the plural is formed by adding either [-s], [-z] or [-əz] to the end of nouns.

_____ Every language has a way of forming questions.

_____ Speakers of Canadian English know that the different vowel sounds in the words **bat, bet, but,** and **bit** are crucial to their meanings.

REVIEW! REVIEW!   Make sure you understand the terms listed below.

- creativity
- descriptive grammar
- grammar
- generality
- inaccessibility
- linguistic competence
- mutability
- native speaker
- parity
- prescriptive grammar

- specialized brain areas
- speech breathing
- speech organs
- universality

QUESTIONS? PROBLEMS? DIFFICULTIES?

_____

_____

_____

_____

_____

_____

_____

_____

_____

_____

_____

_____

_____

_____

CHAPTER 2. PHONETICS:
THE SOUNDS OF LANGUAGE

Phonetics is the study of the articulation and perception of speech sounds. The following are important topics and concepts found in this section.

1. [vowkʰəl trækt]
2. [sawnd klæsəz]
3. [kʰansənənt artʰɪkjulejʃən]
4. [æspəreʃən]
5. [vawəl artʰɪkjulejʃən]
6. [ɪntʰərnæʃənəl fənɛtʰɪk ælfəbɛt] ([aj pʰiej])
7. [sɛgmɛnts]
8. [trænskrɪpʃən]
9. [suprəsɛgmɛntʰəlz]
10. [prowsɛsəz]

By the end of this section, you'll be able to translate the above phonetic transcription (with ease) into standard English.

In "plain" English, the topics we will be discussing in phonetics are:

1. Vocal Tract
2. Sound Classes
3. Consonant Articulation
4. Aspiration
5. Vowel Articulation
6. International Phonetic Alphabet (IPA)
7. Segments
8. Transcription
9. Suprasegmentals
10. Processes

SOUNDS AND PHONETIC TRANSCRIPTION

Human language contains a finite number of speech sounds, or phones. The speech sounds found in language are transcribed using the symbols found in the International Phonetic Alphabet (IPA). Each symbol in this alphabet represents one and only one speech sound. Each speech sound found in language corresponds to one and only one IPA symbol. Since symbols represent sounds, the same symbols can be used in whatever language that sound occurs in.

It is important to remember that IPA symbols represent sounds and not how that sound is spelled in a particular language. To indicate this difference, symbols are enclosed in [ ] brackets. Don't forget to use them!

UNITS OF REPRESENTATION

There are three units of linguistic representation that are relevant to the study of speech sounds. Segments are discussed in this chapter, features and syllables in the next.

Segments: A segment is an individual speech sound. Each symbol in IPA represents a segment.

Features: A feature is a single aspect of articulation. Individual segments are comprised of a number of features. Taken together, these features make up the articulation of the segment.

Syllables: Segments can also combine with each other to form a larger unit called a syllable. Syllables, therefore, consist of one or more segments.

REMINDER!

The focus in this chapter is on learning the IPA symbols corresponding to the vowel and consonant sounds of English. Many, but not all of these sounds are found in other languages. In addition, there are many sounds that do not occur in English, but which are found in other languages. For more information on some of these sounds, their descriptions, and their IPA symbols, please refer to

• Table 2.28 and Table 2.29 in the text, **AND**
• www.pearsoned.ca/text/ogrady/phonetics/other

THE VOCAL TRACT

On the diagram below, label the lungs, trachea, larynx, pharynx, oral cavity, nasal cavity and the velum.

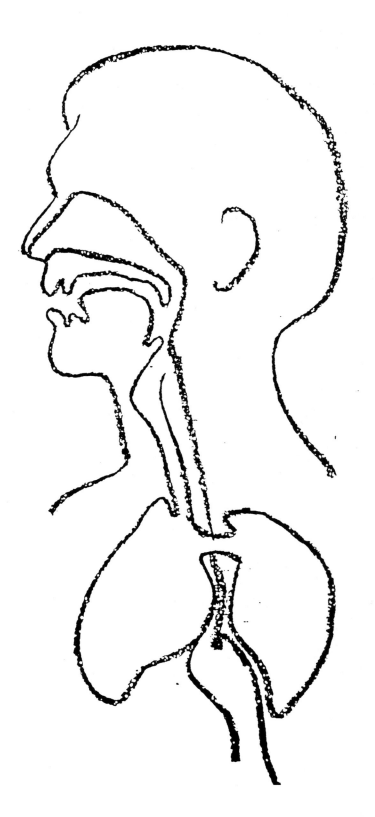

SOUND CLASSES

Sounds produced with the vocal tract can be divided into three major classes: consonants, vowels, and glides. Each class of sounds shares some phonetic properties. The defining characteristics of each class are given below.

⇒ **Consonants.**   Consonants are sounds which can be either voiced or voiceless and which are made with a narrow or complete obstruction in the vocal tract. This is an articulatory characteristic of consonant sounds.

⇒ **Vowels.**   Vowels are sounds which are typically voiced and which are made with little obstruction in the vocal tract. Vowels tend to be more sonorous than consonants. As a result, we perceive vowels as louder and longer lasting. This is an acoustic characteristic of vowels. Vowels are also classified as syllabic sounds, meaning that they can function as the nucleus of a syllable.

⇒ **Glides.**   Glides are sounds that have characteristics of both consonants and vowels. They are sometimes called semivowels or semiconsonants. Glides are like vowels in their articulation, but are like consonants in that they never function as the nucleus of a syllable.

Exercise!   Each of the following words has one or more letters underlined. The underlined letters correspond to one sound. Identify this sound as a consonant, vowel, or glide. The first is done for you!

1. rottweiler   _____consonant_____

2. through   _____

3. lovely   _____

4. year   _____

5. myth   _____

6. whistle   _____

7. suffer   _____

8. judge   _____

ARTICULATORY DESCRIPTIONS

All sounds, regardless of whether they are consonants, vowels, or glides, are described in terms of how they are articulated. This information is contained in the sound's articulatory description. Every sound has one and only one articulatory description. And every articulatory description corresponds to one symbol in the International Phonetic Alphabet (IPA). Consonants and glides are described differently from vowels.

Consonant Articulation

There are three parameters necessary to describe consonant (and glide) articulation:

1. Glottal State
2. Place of Articulation
3. Manner of Articulation

Glottal State refers to whether a sound is voiced or voiceless. Place of Articulation refers to where in the vocal tract an obstruction occurs. Manner of Articulation refers to how the airflow is modified at the place of articulation.

Vowel Articulation

Four parameters are necessary to describe vowels:

1. Tongue Height
2. Tongue Position
3. Tenseness
4. Lip Position

Tongue Height and Tongue Position are used to describe tongue placement. Tenseness refers to the amount of constriction in the vocal tract muscles when the sound is articulated. Lip Position refers to whether the lips are rounded or not.

QUICK REMINDER

For every articulatory description, you need to be able to provide the corresponding phonetic symbol:

$$\text{e.g., voiceless bilabial stop} \quad \rightarrow \quad [p]$$

For every phonetic symbol, you need to be able to provide the corresponding articulatory description:

$$\text{e.g., } [e] \quad \rightarrow \quad \text{mid front tense unrounded vowel}$$

PLACES OF ARTICULATION

On the diagram below, identify all the places of articulation as well as the five areas of the tongue.

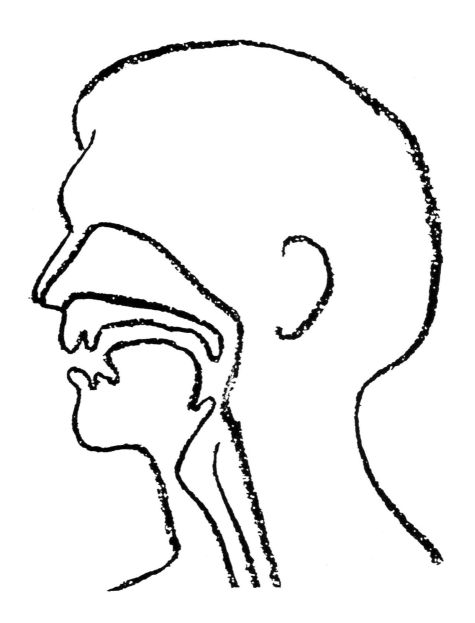

CANADIAN ENGLISH CONSONANT CHART

Fill in the chart below with the symbols corresponding to the consonant and glide sounds of Canadian English. Put a box around the group of fricatives and affricates described as "strident".

		PLACE OF ARTICULATION							
MANNER OF ARTICULATION	GLOTTAL STATE	Bilabial	Labiodental	Interdental	Alveolar	Alveopalatal	Velar	Glottal
Stop	voiceless							
Stop	voiced							
Fricative	voiceless							
Fricative	voiced							
Affricate	voiceless							
Affricate	voiced							
Nasal	voiced							
Liquid a. lateral	voiced							
Liquid b. retroflex	voiced							
Glide	voiced							

ASPIRATION

Sometimes when voiceless stops are pronounced, they are produced with a small puff of air. This puff of air is called aspiration and is represented as [ʰ]. Pronounce the words in the boxes below, paying close attention to the first sound, and see if you can tell when aspiration does and does not occur. You can feel this extra release of air by putting your hand close to your mouth as you produce the words.

ASPIRATED VOICELESS STOPS	
[pʰ]	pit punk
[tʰ]	take tab
[kʰ]	kill car

UNASPIRATED VOICELESS STOPS	
[p]	spit spunk
[t]	stake stab
[k]	skill scar

Voiceless stops in English can be both aspirated and unaspirated. Aspiration occurs when there is a delay in the voicing of the vowel after the voiceless stop. This delay occurs in words such as 'pit', 'take', and 'kill' because there is not enough time after the release of the voiceless stop to vibrate the vocal folds for the vowel articulation. The vowel, therefore, is not immediately voiced, and it is this initial voicelessness that is perceived as a puff of air. In words such as 'spit', 'stake', and 'skill', there is no delay in voicing, and therefore no aspiration. The delay does not occur because the presence of an extra sound provides the time necessary to get the vocal folds into position to immediately start voicing the vowel when the stop is released.

Practice!   Pronounce the following words, and put a check mark beside those words containing aspirated voiceless stops.

1. scratch _____

2. talk _____

3. segments _____

4. pending _____

5. stripe _____

6. careful _____

FACIAL DIAGRAMS FOR CONSONANTS

There are four important parts to either completing or deciphering facial diagrams for consonants.

Voicing / Voicelessness. Voicing is shown by two wavy lines where the larynx would be. Voiceless sounds are represented by two lines shaped like an ellipse.

Voiced   Voiceless

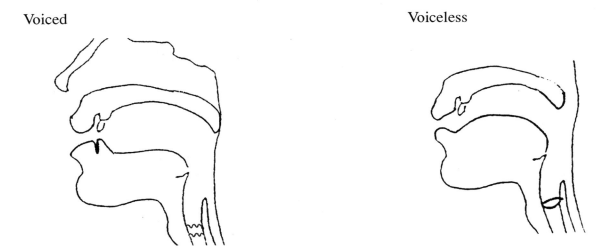

Place of Articulation. The narrowest point in the airstream passage is the place of articulation.

Manner of Articulation. If no air escapes past a given articulator (i.e., a stop), then the articulator must touch the place of articulation. If the air does escape (i.e., a fricative), then there is a space between the articulator and the place of articulation. If the sound is an affricate, then the diagram is shown with the articulator touching the place of articulation and an arrow indicating the direction in which the articulator moves.

Stop   Fricative   Affricate

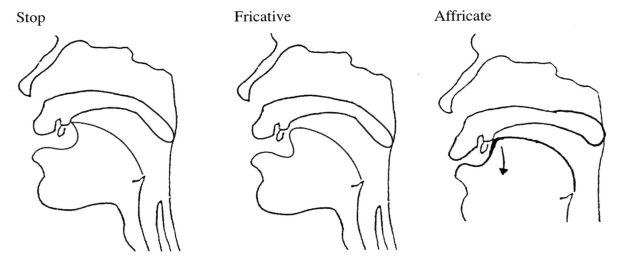

Nasal Passage. For oral sounds, the nasal passage is closed, while for nasal sounds the nasal passage is open.

Complete the following diagrams so that each of the sounds listed below is depicted.

1. [s]   3. [ʧ]   5. [g]
2. [p]   4. [n]   6. [ð]

To complete the diagrams, you must:

- Draw in the glottal state: either voiced or voiceless.
- Draw in the lips: either closed or open.
- Draw the tongue to the place of articulation and to the manner of articulation.
- Draw in the velum: either raised or lowered.

The first sound has been done for you.

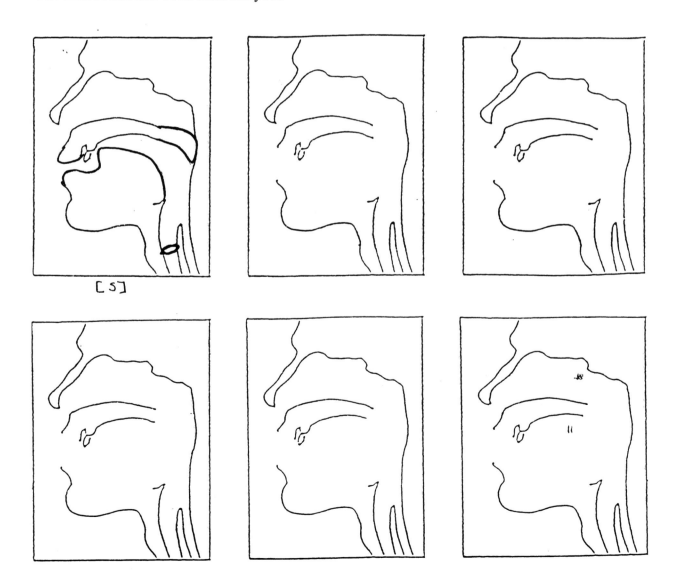

[s]

For each drawing presented below, there is only one sound that could be produced by the vocal tract position. You are to figure out which consonant sound is represented and write the phonetic symbol for that sound between square brackets below the drawing.

Make sure that you pay attention to voicing, place and manner of articulation and to the position of the velum.

The first drawing has been labelled for you.

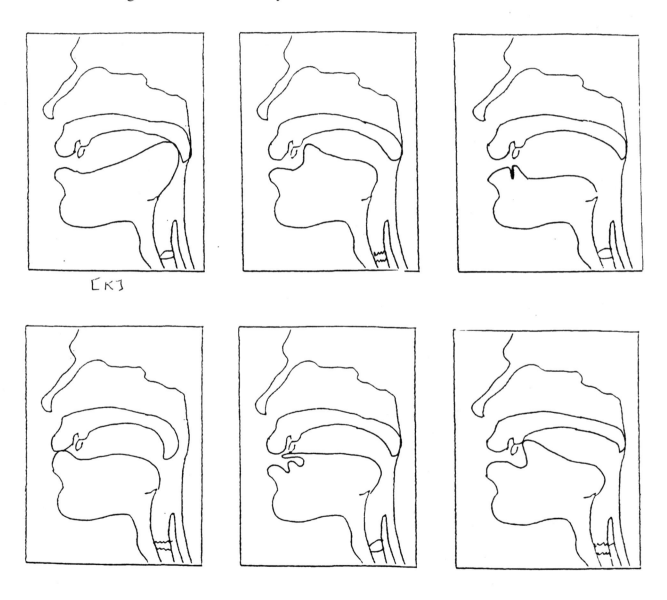

[K]

CANADIAN ENGLISH VOWEL CHART

Fill in the chart below with the phonetic symbols corresponding to both the simple vowels and diphthongs found in Canadian English.

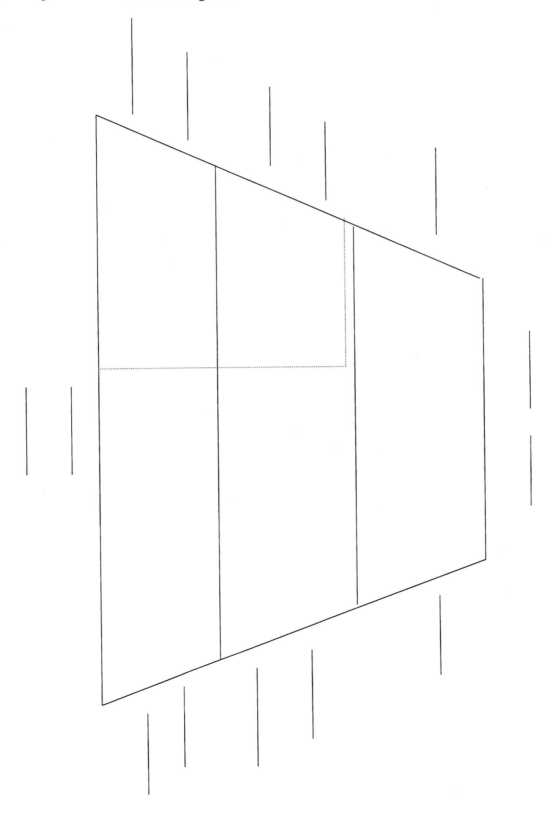

FACIAL DIAGRAMS FOR VOWELS

There are four important parts to either completing or deciphering facial diagrams for vowels.

Voicing. Vowels are always voiced. As on facial diagrams for consonants, voicing is shown by two wavy lines where the larynx would be.

Nasal Passage. For oral vowels, the nasal passage is closed, while for nasal vowels, the nasal passage is open.

Lip Position. Vowels are either rounded or unrounded. For rounded vowels, the lips are closer together, while for unrounded vowels, the lips are more spread apart.

Unrounded:

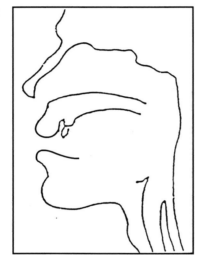

Rounded:

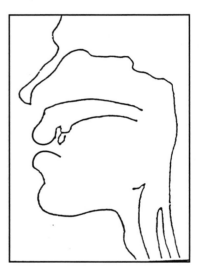

Tongue Placement. The height and position of the tongue determine the particular vowel articulation being depicted. For example, if the front of the tongue is high in the mouth, then a high front vowel results. Or, if the main body of the tongue is neither high nor low, then a mid central vowel results. Or, if the back of the tongue is low, then a low back vowel results.

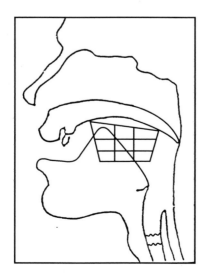
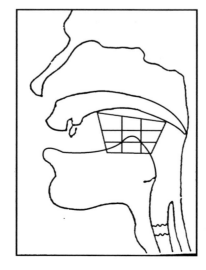
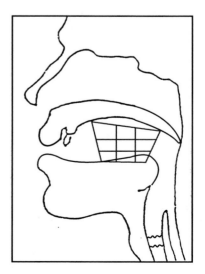

Complete the following diagrams so that each of the sounds listed below are depicted.
1. [æ]   2. [ʌ]   3. [ĩ]

To complete the diagrams, you must:

- Draw in the glottal state.
- Draw in the velum: either raised or lowered.
- Draw in the lips: either rounded or unrounded.
- Draw the appropriate portion of the tongue to the appropriate height.

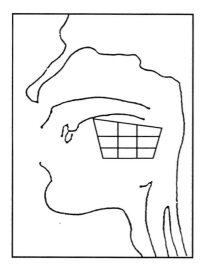 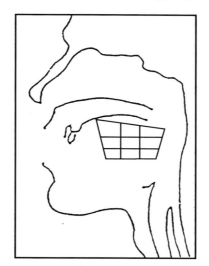 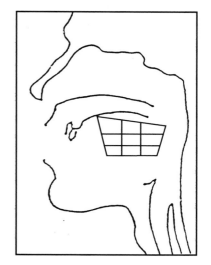

For each drawing presented below, determine which vowel sound is represented and write the phonetic symbol for that sound between the brackets below the drawing.

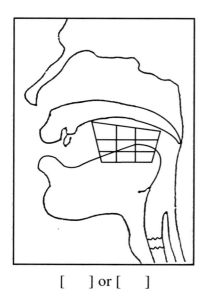 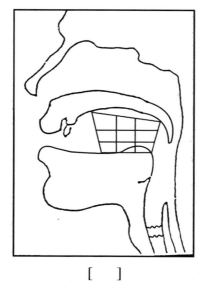 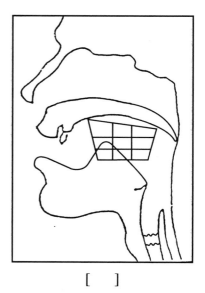

[   ] or [   ]   [   ]   [   ]

SEGMENTS

To successfully transcribe words, you need to be able to identify individual sounds. An individual speech sound (or phone) is called a segment, and each segment is represented by a symbol in the phonetic alphabet. Words typically consist of a number of different speech sounds. To transcribe, you need to determine not only the number of speech sounds in a word, but also what those speech sounds are. But, don't be fooled by spelling! Each of the following boxes illustrates a reason why we can't rely on spelling to determine the number of speech sounds in an English word.

Some words, letters or combinations of letters have more than one speech sound associated with them. In each of the example sets below, determine if the underlined letter (or letters) is pronounced the same way for all the words presented.

⇒   'o'   as in   h<u>o</u>t   ech<u>o</u>   w<u>o</u>man

⇒   'c'   as in   <u>c</u>areful   <u>c</u>entury

⇒   'ou'   as in   sh<u>ou</u>ld   t<u>ou</u>gh   s<u>ou</u>nd

---

Sometimes one speech sound can be represented using different letters or combinations of letters. In each of the example sets below, determine if the underlined letter(s) have the same or different speech sounds.

⇒   thr<u>ough</u>   cl<u>ue</u>   sh<u>oe</u>   t<u>oo</u>

⇒   r<u>ea</u>l   s<u>ee</u>   sorr<u>y</u>   Sh<u>ei</u>la

⇒   str<u>aw</u>   t<u>a</u>lk   f<u>ou</u>ght   l<u>o</u>st

Many words in English contain double letters. Double letters do not necessarily mean that there are two speech sounds. Say each of the words below and determine if you pronounce the double letter twice.

str<u>ee</u>t   b<u>oo</u>k   mi<u>tt</u>en   ki<u>ll</u>er

Finally, many words in English contain silent letters. These are letters which we do not pronounce and which therefore do not correspond to a speech sound. Say each of the words below and determine if you pronounce all of the letters.

knife   leave   pneumonia   catch

The lesson is . . . when you are transcribing words, you need to forget about spelling!

Practice! Practice!   To get ready for transcription, try the following exercises.

1. Determine the number of speech sounds in each of the following words.

    a. thing _____   d. phosphate _____

    b. comb _____   e. scene _____

    c. psychic _____   f. fright _____

2. Give the phonetic symbol for the first sound in each of the following words.

    a. Thomas _____   d. knee _____

    b. unemployed _____ e. choice _____

    c. committee _____ f. ease _____

3. Give the phonetic symbol for the last sound in each of the following words.

    a. laugh _____   d. lamb _____

    b. sang _____   e. use _____

    c. bow _____   f. choice _____

[trænskrɪpʃən tajm]

SYLLABIC CONSONANTS

r	[r] for the 'r' sound in 'real', 'right', etc. [ər], [r̩], or [ɚ] for the syllabic 'r' sound in 'butte<u>r</u>', 'bi<u>r</u>d', 'pu<u>rr</u>', etc. [ɾ] for the 't' sound in words like 'bu<u>tt</u>er', 'wri<u>t</u>er', 'pu<u>tt</u>er', 'po<u>tt</u>er', etc.
l	[l] for the 'l' sound in 'light', 'pill', 'please', etc. [əl] or [l̩] for the syllabic 'l' in 'bott<u>le</u>', 'pudd<u>le</u>', 'pood<u>le</u>', etc.
m	[m̩] for the syllabic 'm' in 'bott<u>om</u>', 'wins<u>ome</u>', etc. [m] for any other 'm' sound
n	[n̩] for the syllabic 'n' in 'butt<u>on</u>', 'hidd<u>en</u>', etc. [n] for any other 'n' sound

VOWELS

The mid tense vowels have an off-glide in phonetic transcription only: phonetic transcription: [ej], [ow]   phonemic transcription: /e/, /o/

Vowels before [r]:   [bir]   beer   [bowr] boar   [bejr]   bear   [bɑr]   bar   [bur]   boor   [bər], [br̩], or [bɚ]   burr

SCHWA AND WEDGE

<u>Schwa [ə]</u>	<u>Wedge [ʌ]</u>

– used for unstressed vowels
     e.g., [əbawt] 'about'
 – found before [r]
     e.g., [bərd] 'bird'
 – used for the words 'the' and 'a'
	– used when there is some degree of stress on the vowel
	     e.g., [sʌpər] 'supper'
	 – is not found before [r]

ASPIRATION

p,t,k	use [pʰ,tʰ,kʰ] for any 'p', 't', 'k' sound that occurs at the beginning of a syllable followed by a vowel that receives some degree of stress. e.g., [pʰæt] 'pat', [tʰɑt] 'taught', [kʰejk] 'cake' [əpʰír] 'appear', [ətʰǽk] 'attack'
	use [p, t, k] for any other 'p', 't', 'k' sound. e.g., [splæt] 'splat', [stɑp] 'stop', [skejt] 'skate'

CANADIAN RAISING

Phonetic Transcription:
 	
  [aj] and [aw] before voiced consonants or when not followed by any consonant
    e.g., [bajd], [laj] 'bide' and 'lie',   [lawd], [baw] 'loud' and 'bough'
  [ʌj] and [ʌw] before voiceless consonants
    e.g., [bʌjt] 'bite', [lʌwt] 'lout'

Phonemic Transcription: /aj/ and /aw/ in all environments

[trænskrɪpʃən ɛksərsajzəz]

Transcribe the following words as you would say them in normal everyday speech. Remember to include brackets and remember to forget spelling!! Watch out for syllabic consonants!

1. craft

2. rich

3. thought

4. sigh

5. tape

6. had

7. health

8. vague

9. exit

10. azure

11. rooster

12. sugar

13. frog

14. instead

15. unit

16. paddle

17. bottom

18. question

19. angel

20. church

Vowel Practice!   Remember that the tense mid vowels have an off-glide in phonetic transcription.

1. key	2. cheese	3. bone
4. due	5. ate	6. east
7. loaf	8. wheeze	9. mainsheet
10. made	11. through	12. throw

More Vowels! This time watch out for vowels before 'r' sounds.

1. cheer	2. there	3. chair
4. car	5. star	6. score
7. sir	8. her	9. floor
10. oar	11. horse	12. course
13. heart	14. hard	15. harm
16. sharp	17. shirt	18. thwart

Practice with diphthongs.   Transcribe the following words as you would in normal everyday speech. Watch out for those diphthongs!!

1. voice	2. trial	3. bicycle
4. hour	5. oily	6. price
7. eyes	8. prize	9. embroider
10. sight	11. sigh	12. sighed
13. prowl	14. counter	15. ice
16. knifed	17. down	18. daze

Remember … transcription takes a lot of practice!

Practice with schwa and wedge.   In this one, pay close attention to the schwa and wedge sounds. You might want to determine which vowel gets primary stress to help you out.

1. sludge

2. thunder

3. hung

4. quality

5. behave

6. oven

7. luck

8. separate

9. stuff

10. nation

11. announce

12. understand

One more try!   This one has everything in it!! Again, transcribe as you would in normal everyday speech. Watch out . . . they get harder!

1. days

2. agitate

3. gnome

4. Xerox

5. roast

6. sixths

7. guess

8. thumb

9. masculine

10. yellow

11. bargain

12. precious

13. science

14. machine

15. formula

16. motorcycle

17. surrounded

18. comedy

19. extinguish

20. costume

21. graduate

22. implement

23. writer

24. irrigate

25. isolate

26. timetable

27. unforgivable

28. frighten

29. lemonade

30. called

Reverse transcription.   Give the correctly spelled English word for each of the following transcriptions.

1. [liʒər]

2. [ʃaj]

3. [pʰajp]

4. [æks]

5. [swit]

6. [safənd]

7. [wərði]

8. [tʰub]

9. [fowni]

10. [wʌns]

11. [tʃojs]

12. [stætʃuw]

13. [ʃejd]

14. [mɛnʃən]

15. [skwɛr]

PRACTICE WITH SOUNDS

Each of the following groups of sounds contains at least one shared phonetic property. Phonetic properties include such things as voice, place of articulation, manner of articulation, tongue height, lip position, etc. For each group of sounds, state the phonetic properties that the sounds have in common. Include as many as possible. The first is done for you.

1. [b, d, g] _____ voiced stops _____

2. [v, d, m] _____

3. [s, ʧ, ʒ] _____

4. [j, ɾ, n] _____

5. [ɑ, o, ʊ] _____

6. [æ, ɪ, ɛ] _____

Groups of sounds that share phonetic properties are called natural classes.

SUPRASEGMENTALS

Suprasegmentals refer to inherent properties that are part of all sounds regardless of their place or manner of articulation. The three main suprasegmentals are pitch, length, and stress. Pitch is further divided into tone and intonation.

Pitch: Tone Languages are languages in which pitch movement is used to signal differences in meaning. Mandarin Chinese is a good example. Tone languages may use register and/or contour tones. A register tone is a level pitch, while a contour tone is a moving pitch.

Intonation is pitch movement that is not related to differences in word meaning. For example, rising pitch is often used to signal a question or an incomplete utterance, and falling intonation a statement or a complete utterance.

Length: Long vowels and consonants are sounds whose articulation simply takes longer relative to other vowels and consonants. Length is indicated with a [ː]. German is an example of a language having long and short vowels. Italian is an example of a language having long and short consonants.

Stress: Stress is associated with vowels. Stressed vowels are vowels that are perceived as more prominent than other vowels. The most prominent vowel receives primary stress. Primary stress is usually indicated with a [´].

PROCESSES

Processes describe articulatory adjustments that occur during speech. Processes typically function to make words easier to articulate. Processes also occur to make speech easier to perceive. The main types of processes are:

1. Assimilation   4. Epenthesis

2. Dissimilation   5. Metathesis

3. Deletion   6. Vowel Reduction

The boxes below define and illustrate the different articulatory processes found in language.

ASSIMILATION

Assimilation involves sounds changing to become more like nearby sounds. While there are many different kinds of assimilation, in general, assimilation can be divided into three main types:

1. Assimilation for Voice:
    – A sound takes on the same voice as a nearby sound
    – Includes: voicing
                  devoicing

2. Assimilation for Place of Articulation:
    – A sound takes on the same place of articulation as a nearby sound.
    – Includes: palatalization
                  homorganic nasal assimilation . . . and more!

3. Assimilation for Manner of Articulation:
    – A sound takes on the same manner of articulation as a nearby sound
    – Includes: nasalization
                  flapping (tapping) . . . and more!

In addition ... some types of assimilation, such as nasalization, can be either regressive or progressive. In regressive assimilation, a segment takes on some characteristic of the following segment. That is, a sound is influenced by what comes after it. In progressive assimilation, a segment takes on some characteristic of the preceding segment. That is, a sound is influenced by what comes before it.

DISSIMILATION

A sound changes to become less like a nearby sound so that the resulting sequence of sounds is easier to pronounce, e.g., fifths: [fɪfθs] → [fɪfts]

DELETION

The process of deletion simply removes a sound from a phonetic context. Deletion frequently occurs in rapid speech, e.g., fifths: [fɪfθs] → [fɪfs]

EPENTHESIS

The process of epenthesis adds a segment to a phonetic context. Epenthesis is common in casual speech, e.g., warmth: [warmθ] → [warmpθ]

METATHESIS

Metathesis is a process that changes the order of segments. Metathesis is common in the speech of young children, e.g., prescribe → perscribe

VOWEL REDUCTION

In vowel reduction, vowels move to a more central position when they are in unstressed syllables. That is, a vowel is pronounced as a full vowel when in a stressed syllable, and as a schwa when in an unstressed syllable.

Identifying processes ... To identify processes, you need to look for differences between the starting and ending pronunciations.

⇒ If a sound is missing, **deletion** has occurred.
⇒ If a sound has been added, **epenthesis** has occurred.
⇒ If the order of sounds has changed, **metathesis** has occurred.
⇒ If a sound has changed, you need to determine if either **assimilation** or **dissimilation** has occurred. To do this:
  • determine the phonetic property that has changed (voice, place, or manner of articulation).
  • compare this phonetic property with the phonetic properties of the nearby sounds.
  • if the changed phonetic property matches a phonetic property of a nearby sound, then **assimilation** has occurred. The phonetic property that matches will tell you the specific type of assimilation that has occurred.
  • if the phonetic properties do not match, then **dissimilation** has occurred.

Remember ... for assimilation, you also need to be able to identify when processes such as nasalization or place of articulation assimilation are regressive and when they are progressive. To determine this, you need to look at whether the influencing sound comes before (progressive) or after (regressive) the sound that is undergoing the change.

An example ... Consider the following example.

prince: [prɪns]   →   [prɪ̃nts]

In the above example, [t] occurs in the final pronunciation but not the starting; therefore, epenthesis has occurred. As well, [ɪ] has changed to [ɪ̃]. Remember that [~] indicates a nasalized sound. The vowel, therefore, has changed from an oral to a nasal sound, and since the following sound is a nasal, assimilation, in particular nasalization, has occurred. The influencing sound is the following nasal, meaning that the nasalization is regressive. So, the change in the pronunciation of the word 'prince' from [prɪns] to [prɪ̃nts] involves two processes: epenthesis and regressive nasalization.

Try these!   Identify the process(es) at work in each of the following:

1. sibilant: [sɪbələnt]   →   [sɪləbənt]   _____

2. Peter: [pʰitər]   →   [pʰidər]   _____

3. puddle: [pʰʌdəl]   →   [pʰʌɾəl]   _____

4. good bye: [gʊdbaj]   →   [gʊ̃mbaj]   _____

5. sixths: [sɪksθs]   →   [sɪksts]   _____

REVIEW EXERCISES

1. For each part of the vocal tract, give its corresponding role in speech production.

    a. lungs   _____

    b. larynx   _____

    c. velum   _____

2. Give the articulatory term describing sounds made at each of the following places of articulation.

    a. lips   _____

    b. hard palate   _____

    c. uvula   _____

    d. larynx   _____

3. Give the phonetic symbol for each of the following articulatory descriptions.

    a. [   ]   voiceless glottal stop

    b. [   ]   high front unrounded tense vowel

    c. [   ]   voiced bilabial nasal

    d. [   ]   voiceless interdental fricative

4. Give the articulatory description that corresponds to each of the following phonetic symbols.

    a. [æ]   _____

    b. [v]   _____

    c. [j]   _____

    d. [ʌ]   _____

5. Give the phonetic symbol for the vowel sound in each of the following English words.

a. stool_____   d. pot _____

b. sight_____   e. sit _____

c. meet_____   f. put _____

6. Transcribe the following words in normal everyday speech. Mark primary stress.

a. scorned   f. duplicate

b. discovery   g. dictate

c. explosion   h. occupied

d. genius   i. informative

e. macaroni   j. idolize

7. For each of the following groups of sounds, circle the sound that does not belong and state a phonetic property which the remaining sounds share. There may be more than one possible answer!

a. [f ð v m] _____

b. [d t n g] _____

c. [ɑ o ɪ u] _____

8. Identify all the processes at work in each of the following:

a. wash: [wɑʃ] → [warʃ]   _____

b. winter: [wɪntər] → [wɪ̃nər]   _____

c. clear: [kl̥ir] → [kəlir]   _____

d. sandwich: [sændwɪtʃ] → [sæ̃mwɪtʃ] _____

e. animal: [ænɪməl] → [æ̃mĩnəl]   _____

REVIEW! REVIEW!   Make sure you know:

- the different parts of the vocal tract
- the difference between voiced and voiceless sounds
- the difference between nasal and oral sounds
- the characteristics of consonants, glides and vowels
- the places and manners of articulation for consonant sounds
- the different tongue placements required to describe vowels
- the difference between tense and lax, and rounded and unrounded vowels
- the symbols and articulatory descriptions for English consonants
- the strident fricatives and affricates
- the symbols and articulatory descriptions for English vowels
- when and why aspiration occurs
- how to complete and decipher facial diagrams
- how to identify natural classes
- how to identify processes
- the suprasegmentals of tone, intonation, length, and stress
- transcription, transcription, transcription!!

QUESTIONS? PROBLEMS? DIFFICULTIES?

_____

_____

_____

_____

_____

_____

_____

_____

_____

_____

_____

CHAPTER 3. PHONOLOGY:
THE FUNCTION & PATTERNING OF SOUNDS

Phonology is the study of how sounds vary and pattern in language. The important terms, concepts and topics of discussion within this chapter include:

1. contrast
2. minimal pairs
3. complementary distribution
4. phonemes and allophones
5. phonology problems
6. near minimal pairs and free variation
7. phonetic and phonemic transcription
8. syllables
9. features
10. rules and statements
11. derivations and rule-ordering

Since we will be dealing with many languages besides English, you will come across some phonetic symbols which have not been discussed. Articulatory descriptions will be provided for these unfamiliar sounds!

CONTRAST

Segments are said to contrast when their presence alone is responsible for forms having different meanings. Both consonant and vowel segments may contrast with each other. Which segments contrast with each other varies from language to language, as the following examples show.

	Language	**Segments**	**Forms**
Consonants	English	[kʰ] [g]	[kʰæp] 'cap' vs [gæp] 'gap'
	Khmer	[kʰ] [k]	[kʰat] 'to polish' vs [kat] 'to cut'
Vowels	English	[i] [æ]	[bit] 'beet' vs [bæt] 'bat'
		[ow] [u]	[kʰowd] 'code' vs [kʰud] 'cooed'
	Japanese	[i] [iː]	[tori] 'bird' vs [toriː] 'shrine gate'
		[o] [oː]	[kibo] 'scale' vs [kiboː] 'hope'

Determining which segments contrast is a first step in phonological analysis!

MINIMAL PAIRS

A minimal pair is defined as two phonetic forms which differ by one segment that is in the same position in both forms, and which have different meanings. Minimal pairs tell us that sounds contrast.

For each of the following, answer Y if the paired words constitute a minimal pair and N if they do not. Make sure you pay attention to the meanings given in ''!

a. [bækt] 'towel'   and   [pækd] 'cloth'   _____

b. [ʧogʊr] 'necklace'   and   [ʧogʊl] 'bracelet'   _____

c. [telʌm] 'book'   and   [tɛlʌm] 'book'   _____

d. [kətɑge] 'letter'   and   [kətɑge] 'paper'   _____

For each of the following pairs of English consonant phonemes, find two minimal pairs. Wherever possible, one pair should show one contrast in initial position and the other, one in final position. The first pair is done as an example for you. Don't be fooled by spelling!

a. / p : b /   _____paste : baste_____   _____rope : robe_____

b. / t : d /   _____   _____

c. / k : g /   _____   _____

d. / f : v /   _____   _____

e. / s : z /   _____   _____

f. / m : n /   _____   _____

g. / r : l /   _____   _____

h. / t : θ /   _____   _____

i. / ʧ : ʤ /   _____   _____

j. / p : f /   _____   _____

COMPLEMENTARY DISTRIBUTION

Not all segments found in a language contrast with each other. Some segments are in complementary distribution. Two phonetically similar segments are in complementary distribution when they never occur in the same phonetic environment. The term "environment" refers to the phonetic context in which the segments occur.

The following example will help illustrate the nature of complementary distribution.

Environment:		Before Nasals	After Nasals	Before Oral Sounds
English	Nasal Vowels	YES	NO	NO
	Oral Vowels	NO	YES	YES
Scots Gaelic	Nasal Vowels	YES	YES	NO
	Oral Vowels	NO	NO	YES

In English...   nasal and oral vowels are in complementary distribution. Nasal vowels only occur before nasal consonants, while oral vowels occur after nasal consonants and also before oral sounds.   Oral vowels are designated as occurring elsewhere, since there are always more oral sounds than nasal sounds in a language.

In Scots Gaelic...   nasal and oral vowels are also in complementary distribution, but this distribution is different from what is found in English. In Scots Gaelic, nasal vowels occur both before and after nasal consonants, and oral vowels occur before oral sounds. However, nasal vowels may occur before oral sounds, but only if they are preceded by a nasal consonant.

As you can see, the occurrence of nasal and oral vowels in both English and Scots Gaelic is predictable.

Native speakers of a language think of segments that are in complementary distribution as instances of the same sound. We say that these segments are phonetically different, since they have different articulations. However, since they do not contrast and since they occur in predictable environments, they are phonologically the same segment.

THINK...   of a language in which nasal and oral vowels are not in complementary distribution, but rather are contrastive!

PHONEMES AND ALLOPHONES

Phonemes and allophones are two units of representation used in phonology. These are used to capture native speakers' knowledge about how sounds pattern in their language.

PHONEME means ...   1. The way in which sounds are stored in the mind.

2. The contrastive phonological units of a language.

3. Underlying Representation.

ALLOPHONE means...   1. The way in which sounds are pronounced.

2. The predictable variants of the language's phonological units.

3. Surface Representation.

Contrastive sounds belong to separate phonemes and are represented on two levels.

Phonemic: / /   / /

Phonetic: [ ]   [ ]

Phonetically distinct, but phonologically the same sounds belong to the same phoneme and are also represented on two levels.

Phonemic: / /

Phonetic: [ ]   [ ]

QUICK REMINDER!!

Don't forget to use / / brackets to indicate phonemes and to use [ ] brackets to indicate allophones.

DETERMINING COMPLEMENTARY DISTRIBUTION

The following exercises are designed to help you understand and determine complementary distribution.

1. The English phoneme /p/ has three allophones: [p]   – unaspirated
                                                      [pʰ] – aspirated
                                                      [p̚] – unreleased

The following list of words gives examples of each phonetic variant.

[p]	[pʰ]	[p̚]
spook	pig	collapse
spirit	police	apt
operate	appear	flipped
hippy	repair	ape
happening		cop
		clap

On the chart below, put a check in the box if the allophone can occur in that environment. The explanation of the different environments is given below.

	#_____	_____#	s_____	_____C	V́_____V	V_____V́
[p]						
[pʰ]						
[p̚]						

Explanation of environments:

#_____	word-initial position	_____#	word-final position
s_____	after [s]	_____C	before a consonant
V́_____V	between vowels (1st vowel is stressed)	V_____V́	between vowels (2nd vowel is stressed)

2. The English phoneme /l/ has (at least) three allophones: [l] – alveolar l
                                                                 [ł] – velarized l
                                                                 [l̩] – syllabic l

The following list of words gives examples of each phonetic variant.

[l]	[ł]	[l̩]
lip	swallow	paddle
love	silly	obstacle
allow	salt	twinkle
malign	ilk	hassle
slip	pull	bushel
slide	meal	hurdle

On the chart below, put a check in the box if the allophone can occur in that environment. An explanation of the environments is given below.

	#____	C____V	V____#	C____#	____C	V́____V	V____V́
[l]							
[ł]							
[l̩]							

Explanation of environments:

#_____   word-initial position

C_____V   between a consonant and a vowel

V_____#   word-final after a vowel

C_____#   word-final after a consonant

_____C   before a consonant

V́_____V   between vowels when the first vowel is stressed

V_____V́   between vowels when the second vowel is stressed

3. Examine the following data from Oneida and determine if the sounds [s] and [z] are or are not in complementary distribution. Note that [sh] represents [s] and [h] and not [ʃ].

[s]		[z]	
[lashet]	let him count	[kawenezuzeʔ]	long words
[laʔsluni]	white men	[khaiize]	I'm taking it along
[loteswatu]	he's been playing	[lazel]	let him drag it
[skahnehtat]	one pine tree	[tahazehteʔ]	he dropped it
[thiskate]	a different one	[tuzahatiteni]	they changed it
[sninuhe]	you buy	[wezake]	she saw you
[wahsnestakeʔ]	you ate corn		

4. Now determine if the sounds [s] and [ʃ] are or are not in complementary distribution. Again, [sh] represents [s] and [h], not [ʃ].

[s]		[ʃ]	
[lashet]	let him count	[ʃjatuheʔ]	you write
[laʔsluni]	white men	[tehʃjaʔk]	let you break
[loteswatu]	he's been playing	[jaʔteʃjatekhahʃjahteʔ]	
[skahnehtat]	one pine tree		they would suddenly
[thiskate]	a different one		separate again
[sninuhe]	you buy		
[wahsnestakeʔ]	you ate corn		

5. Now try this one! Examine the following data from Japanese and determine if the sounds [t], [ʧ] and [ts] are or are not in complementary distribution.

    The symbol [ts] is a single segment representing a voiceless alveolar affricate.

[tatami]	mat	[tsukue]	desk
[tegami]	letter	[ato]	later
[ʧiʧi]	father	[deguʃi]	exit
[ʃita]	under	[tsutsumu]	to wrap
[matsu]	to wait	[kata]	person
[natsu]	summer	[tatemono]	building
[ʧizu]	map	[te]	hand
[koto]	fact	[uʧi]	house
[tomodaʧi]	friend	[otoko]	male
[totemo]	very	[tetsudau]	to help

SOLVING PHONOLOGY PROBLEMS

The basic goal in solving a phonology problem is to determine if the sounds being examined belong to the same phoneme or to separate phonemes.

WHEN ALLOPHONES BELONG TO SEPARATE PHONEMES, THEY ARE:

1. Contrastive/distinctive
2. In unpredictable distribution
3. Easily perceived as different
4. Not necessarily phonetically similar

WHEN ALLOPHONES BELONG TO THE SAME PHONEME, THEY ARE:

1. Non-contrastive/rule-governed
2. In predictable distribution
3. Not easily perceived as different
4. Always phonetically similar

PROBLEM SOLVING FLOWCHART

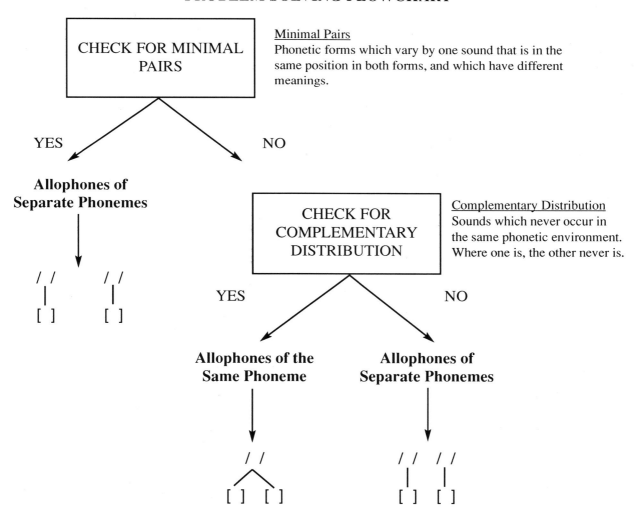

Repeat the above for each pair of sounds you are investigating!

1.   Arabic: [h] and [ʔ]

a.	[ʔuru:b]	wars		e.	[huru:b]	flight
b.	[fahm]	understanding		f.	[faʔm]	coal
c.	[habba]	gust, squall		g.	[ʔabba]	grain, seed
d.	[ha:l]	cardamom		h.	[ʔa:l]	condition

2.   Hebrew: [θ] and [t]   ([x] represents a voiceless velar fricative)

a.	[tafar]	saw		e.	[tannur]	stove
b.	[ʃtaim]	two		f.	[oθax]	you
c.	[iθi]	with me		g.	[teʃaʔ]	nine
d.	[raiθa]	you saw		h.	[tamid]	always

3.   Japanese (modified): [h] and [f]

a.	[higaʃi]	east		f.	[fidui]	old
b.	[heja]	room		g.	[gohan]	cooked rice
c.	[futastu]	two rooms		h.	[hjaku]	100
d.	[haha]	mother		i.	[ʃidoi]	white
e.	[ofudo]	bath		j.	[honto]	really

PROBLEMS! PROBLEMS! PROBLEMS!

The following pages contain data sets from a number of different languages. Some of the data may have been regularized. Each data set contains sufficient data to make valid conclusions about the sounds under consideration. For each data set, do the following:

• state your conclusion (i.e., allophones of the same or separate phonemes)

• provide evidence to support your conclusion

• provide a representation of the phoneme(s)

1. Slovak: [f] and [v]

1.	[vatra]	campfire	4.	[vɔlk]	wolf
2.	[farba]	paint	5.	[feltʃar]	paint
3.	[faːdni]	monotonous	6.	[vedro]	bucket

2. English: [l] and [ɫ]

> **Note:** The English data presented below has been simplified somewhat. For a more challenging (and more accurate) analysis of English [l] and [ɫ], try problem 10 on page 94 of the text!
>
> [~]   When this diacritic appears THROUGH a symbol, it means that the sound has been velarized. [ɫ] is a velarized lateral liquid. It is sometimes called the 'dark l'.

1.	[lɪp]	lip	7.	[fɪlθ]	filth
2.	[lʌvli]	lovely	8.	[waɫgrinz]	Wallgreens
3.	[sɪɫk]	silk	9.	[gɪlt]	guilt
4.	[slajm]	slime	10.	[gowfər]	gopher
5.	[mɪɫk]	milk	11.	[tæɫk]	talc
6.	[kæɫgri]	Calgary	12.	[hiəl]	heal

3. Russian: [a] and [ɑ]

[a]   This symbol represents a low central lax unrounded vowel.

Remember, you want to look for minimal pairs involving the sounds that you have been asked to investigate. There may be other minimal pairs in the data, but you only want those that contain the phones you are asked to examine.

1.	[atəm]	atom	6.	[pɑɫ]	he fell
2.	[dva]	two	7.	[dɑɫ]	he gave
3.	[pɑɫkə]	stick	8.	[dar]	gift
4.	[mas]	ointment	9.	[matə]	mint
5.	[ukrɑɫə]	she stole	10.	[brɑɫ]	he took

4. Korean: [l] and [ř]

[ř]   This symbol represents a flapped [r].
[ʉ]   This symbol represents a high central rounded vowel.

1.	[kal]	dog	11.	[silkwa]	fruit
2.	[kenel]	shade	12.	[mul]	water
3.	[iřumi]	name	13.	[seul]	Seoul
4.	[kiři]	road	14.	[kəřiřo]	to the street
5.	[juŋutʃʉm]	receipt	15.	[sařam]	person
6.	[pal]	leg	16.	[tatʉl]	all of them
7.	[ilkop]	seven	17.	[vəřʉm]	summer
8.	[ipalsa]	barber			
9.	[uři]	we			
10.	[onelppam]	tonight			

5. Inuktitut: [u] and [a]

[q]   This symbol represents a voiceless uvular stop.

1.	[iglumut]	to a house	6. [aniguvit]	if you leave
2.	[ukiaq]	late fall	7. [ini]	place, spot
3.	[iglu]	(snow)house	8. [ukiuq]	winter
4.	[aiviq]	walrus	9. [ani]	female's brother
5.	[pinna]	that one up there	10. [anigavit]	because you leave

6. English: [g], [gʲ] and [gʷ]

[gʲ]   This symbol represents a 'fronted [g]' made with the back of the tongue at or near the hard palate.

[gʷ]   This symbol represents a 'rounded [g]' made with simultaneous lip rounding.

1.	[gɑn]	gone	7. [gʲik]	geek
2.	[gʷufi]	goofy	8. [igər]	eager
3.	[gli]	glee	9. [gejm]	game
4.	[slʌg]	slug	10. [gowfər]	gopher
5.	[grin]	green	11. [gædʒət]	gadget
6.	[rægʷu]	Ragu	12. [gʲis]	geese

7. Sindhi: [p], [b], and [pʰ]

For these three sounds to be allophones of separate phonemes, you must find a minimal pair for:

- [p] and [b]
- [p] and [pʰ], and
- [b] and [pʰ]

You may use the same data item in more than one minimal pair.

1.	[pʌnu]	leaf	7.	[tʌru]	bottom
2.	[vʌdʒu]	opportunity	8.	[kʰʌto]	sour
3.	[ʃʌki]	suspicious	9.	[bʌdʒu]	run
4.	[gʌdo]	dull	10.	[bʌnu]	forest
5.	[dʌru]	door	11.	[bʌtʃu]	be safe
6.	[pʰʌnu]	snakehood	12.	[dʒʌdʒu]	judge

8. Korean: [s], [z], and [ʃ]

1.	[ʃihap]	game	7.	[ʃilsu]	mistake
2.	[ʃipsam]	thirteen	8.	[ʃinho]	signal
3.	[inza]	greetings	9.	[paŋzək]	cushion
4.	[juŋučʉm]	receipt	10.	[ʃesuʃil]	washroom
5.	[son]	hand	11.	[sɔm]	sack
6.	[us]	upper	12.	[sæk]	color

NEAR MINIMAL PAIRS AND FREE VARIATION

<u>Near Minimal Pairs:</u>   Pairs that have segments in nearly identical phonetic environments. They can also be used to establish that sounds contrast.
e.g., Hindi [bara] 'large' and [b̪ari] 'heavy'

<u>Free Variation:</u>   Two sounds which occur in identical phonetic environments, but which do not make a meaning difference.
e.g., English [stap!], [stap˥] and [stapˀ]

For each of the data sets below, determine whether the sounds are allophones of separate phonemes, the same phoneme, or in free variation.

1. Tojolabal (spoken in Mexico):   [k] and [k']

   [']   This diacritic means the sound has been glottalized.

1.	[kisim]	my beard	7.	[sak]	white
2.	[tʃak'a]	chop it down	8.	[k'isin]	warm
3.	[koktit]	our feet	9.	[skutʃu]	he is carrying it
4.	[k'ak]	flea	10.	[k'uutes]	to dress
5.	[p'akan]	hanging	11.	[snika]	he stirred it
6.	[k'aʔem]	sugar cane	12.	[ʔak']	read

2. Kenyang (spoken in Cameroon): [k] and [q]   Then: [b] and [β].

   [q]   This symbol represents a voiceless uvular stop.
   [β]   This symbol represents a voiced bilabial fricative.

1.	[enoq]	tree	7.	[uβit]	person's name
2.	[eβet]	house	8.	[ntʃiβu]	I am buying
3.	[bag]	rope	9.	[etaq]	town
4.	[enok]	tree	10.	[nab]	brother-in-law
5.	[nbat]	knife	11.	[pobrin]	work project
6.	[etak]	town	12.	[ndeβi]	European

PHONETIC AND PHONEMIC TRANSCRIPTION

Phonetic transcription is a representation of normal, everyday speech. That is, it is a representation of pronunciation. Phonetic transcription is always indicated with [ ] brackets. Phonemes represent the knowledge a native speaker has about how sounds pattern in his or her language. We can represent this knowledge using phonemic transcription. Phonemic transcription, as the name suggests, contains only the phonemes of the language and is always indicated with / / brackets.

Since there are two levels of representation (phonetic and phonemic), a language will have two inventories of sounds. The phonetic inventory contains the allophones of the language, while the phonemic inventory contains the phonemes of the language. Allophones are used to transcribe phonetically and phonemes are used to transcribe phonemically.

To understand the difference between phonetic and phonemic transcription, let's reconsider the Russian problem on page 42. Remember that, in Russian, [a] and [ɑ] are allophones of the same phoneme, with [ɑ] occurring before [ɬ], a velarized lateral liquid, and [a] elsewhere. Given this information, we can convert Russian phonetic transcription into Russian phonemic transcription.

	Phonetic		Phonemic	
[mas]	ointment	/mas/	ointment
[ukraɬə]	she stole	/ukraɬə/	she stole
[brɑɬ]	he took	/brɑɬ/	he took

Notice that in the phonemic transcription, only the phoneme /a/ has been used, while in the phonetic transcription the allophones [a] and [ɑ] have both been used. Also notice that in phonetic transcription [ɑ] only ever occurs before [ɬ], while in phonemic transcription /a/ occurs in all environments.

Remember . . .   The main difference between phonetic and phonemic transcription is that phonetic transcription includes both predictable and unpredictable phonetic information, while phonemic transcription includes only the unpredictable information. Anything that is predictable is excluded.

Practice! Practice!   To practice phonemic transcription, go back over the phonology problems on pages 47–50 and page 51, and wherever allophones of the same phoneme were found, convert the first few words in the data set from the phonetic transcription provided into a phonemic transcription. See if you can identify the predictable phonetic property that is missing from the phonemic transcription!

SYLLABLES

A syllable is a unit of representation consisting of one or more segments. There are five pieces of information crucial to understanding syllables, their structure, and their role in phonology. Make sure you know them!

⇒ **Syllables.** A syllable consists of a sonorant element and any associated less sonorous elements. Vowels usually form the core of the syllable, as they are the most sonorant type of sound. The core of a syllable is called the nucleus. Onsets are less sonorant segment(s) that occur before the nucleus, while codas are less sonorant segment(s) occurring after the nucleus.

⇒ **Phonotactics.** Phonotactics is the set of constraints on which segments can occur together. For example, in English, [pl] is an acceptable onset, as in the word 'please', but [tl] is not an acceptable onset: words in English do not begin with this combination of sounds. Phonotactics can vary from language to language.

⇒ **Accidental and Systematic Gaps.** Not all combinations of sounds are found in the words of a language. Accidental gaps refer to non-occurring but possible forms, while systematic gaps refer to the exclusion of certain sequences. For example, the lack of words beginning with [ft] in English is not accidental but systematic, as such a sequence is unacceptable to speakers of the language. In contrast, that English does not have a word such as 'frip' is accidental, since many existing words begin with [fr] (e.g., frog).

⇒ **Syllable Structure.** Syllables have internal structure which is represented above the individual segments comprising the syllable. A syllable (σ) consists of an optional onset (O) and an obligatory rhyme (R). Rhymes consist of a nucleus (N) and an optional coda (Co).

⇒ **Syllable Representations.** There are three, sometimes four, steps to putting together a representation of a syllable. These are illustrated below for the word 'template'.

First: Assign the nucleus, the rhyme, and the syllable node. Vowels (including diphthongs) and syllabic consonants may occupy the nucleus position. (Diphthongs are often diagrammed as a branching nucleus.)

σ   σ
| |
R   R
| |
N   N
| |
t ɛ m p l e t

Second: Assign the onset. These are the segments to the left of the nucleus. Segments assigned to the onset are usually the largest sequence of sounds that can occur at the beginning of a word within a language.

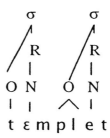

Third: Assign the coda. These are the segments to the right of the nucleus which have not yet been syllabified into an onset.

Open syllables have no coda, while **closed syllables** have a coda.

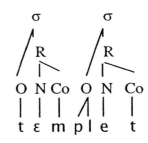

Fourth: As you can see from the representation being constructed, words can consist of a number of syllables. The last step in constructing syllabic representations simply involves combining syllables into words.

This step, however, is frequently omitted.

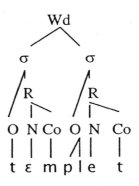

Try this!   Construct a syllable representation for each of the following English words. Remember to transcribe the words first! Underline all open syllables.

1. garden
2. downtown
3. banana

4. twinkle
5. understand
6. beauty

7. lovely
8. satisfy
9. property

Remember...   To always assign onsets before codas.
This reflects a universal preference in language for onsets over codas.

Remember...   That a syllable does not have to have either an onset or a coda.
A syllable, however, must have a nucleus and therefore also a rhyme.

Variation in Syllable Structure . . . Syllable structure can vary from language to language, yet the process for building syllable representations, as outlined above, can still be used.

In the language data below, all syllables have the structure CV(C).[1] This means that all syllables begin with an onset, but do not have to have a coda. That is, codas are optional. Construct syllable representations for following words. The data has already been transcribed for you.

1.   2.   3.

[z i ʧ n o]   [t a g k u]   [s e d n a k u]
     chair   shell   sofa

Syllables and Phonology . . . Syllables are often relevant to stating generalizations about the distribution of allophones. For example, English voiceless aspirated stops are found at the beginning of syllables, and unaspirated stops are found elsewhere. Similarly, phonetic length is predictable in English: vowels are long when followed by a voiced obstruent in the coda position of the same syllable.

The data below is from the same language as above. In this language, stress is predictable, and is marked by a [´] over a vowel. Determine (making reference to syllable structure) where stress occurs.

> Hint: You might want to first syllabify some of the words using the syllabification procedure from above.

1. [fémba]	foot	8. [póbzuʤi]	lizard
2. [hagút]	month	9. [gaʧótfobi]	knee
3. [fezók]	music	10. [talagubiták]	cowboy
4. [waláp]	mole	11. [páfzuliha]	thin
5. [supóspa]	gravy	12. [kéllaboga]	arm
6. [tugábʧo]	stone		
7. [yumayumáp]	armadillo		

---

[1] The language used for these two exercises is a made-up one.

FEATURES

Features represent individual aspects of speech production. Features are usually divided into four categories, as shown below.

Major Class Features	Manner Features
⇒ [+/-consonantal] ⇒ [+/-syllabic] ⇒ [+/-sonorant]	⇒ [+/-continuant] ⇒ [+/-nasal] ⇒ [+/-lateral] ⇒ [+/-delayed release]
Laryngeal Features	**Place Features**
⇒ [+/-voice] ⇒ [+/-spread glottis (SG)] ⇒ [+/-constricted glottis (CG)]	⇒ [LABIAL] 　[+/-round] ⇒ [CORONAL] 　[+/-anterior], [+/-strident] ⇒ [DORSAL] 　[+/-high], [+/-low], [+/-back], 　[+/-tense], [+/-reduced]

Since features represent articulation, they are always enclosed in phonetic (i.e., [ ]) brackets.

Except for [LABIAL], [CORONAL], and [DORSAL], all features are binary and are specified either as plus or minus. [LABIAL], [CORONAL], and [DORSAL] are used to represent the articulator that is active in executing the articulation:

⇒ [LABIAL] for the lips;

⇒ [CORONAL] for the tongue tip or blade; and

⇒ [DORSAL] for the body of the tongue.

All other place features do have plus and minus specifications. These features are used to represent place of articulation features specific to the active articulator. That is, labial sounds are [+/-round]; coronal sounds are [+/-anterior] and [+/-strident]; and dorsal sounds are [+/-high], [+/-low], [+/-back], [+/-tense] and [+/-reduced].

<u>Determining feature representations ...</u>

⇒ **For segments.** Think about the articulatory description for that sound. Begin with the major class features and include in the matrix the appropriate value for each feature, so that when the features are taken together they define whether the segment is a consonant (obstruent or sonorant), a glide, or a vowel. Do the same for the manner, laryngeal, and place features. Remember for the place features, you need to first determine the active articulator, and then the features corresponding to the exact position of that articulator.

[p] is a voiceless bilabial
unaspirated stop

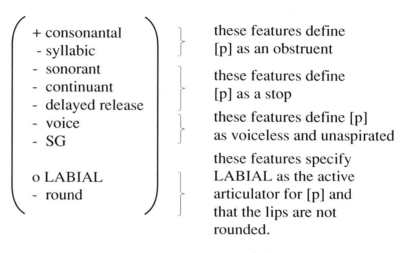

	these features define [p] as an obstruent
+ consonantal	
- syllabic	
- sonorant	these features define [p] as a stop
- continuant	
- delayed release	
- voice	these features define [p] as voiceless and unaspirated
- SG	
o LABIAL	these features specify LABIAL as the active articulator for [p] and that the lips are not rounded.
- round	

⇒ **For natural classes.** Remember that a natural class shares a feature or group of features. Think about the features that the natural class shares. Include in the matrix only those features that all members of the natural class share.

voiceless unaspirated stops
(i.e., [p, t, k])

+ consonantal	these features define all members as obstruents
- syllabic	
- sonorant	these features define all members as stops
- continuant	
- delayed release	
- voice	these features define all members as voiceless and unaspirated
- SG	

Note that place features have not been included in the matrix. This is because [p,t,k] each have a different place of articulation.

⇒ **For allophonic variation.**   Remember that allophones are the predictable variants of phonemes and that their distribution can be described using a rule. Remember as well that rules have three parts: an individual phoneme or class of contrastive sounds, the allophone or change, and the environment in which the change occurs. Include features for each component of the rule. For the allophone, or change, only include the feature that changed from the contrastive sound(s). Some environments such as word- or syllable-initial, or word- or syllable-final, do not need features!

Statement: voiceless unaspirated stops become aspirated syllable-initially.

In feature notation:

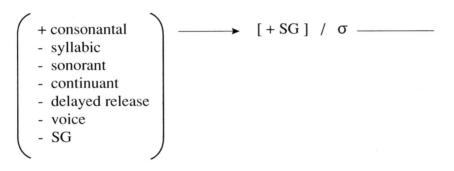

QUICK REMINDER

See pages 81 and 82 in the text for feature matrices for English consonants and vowels. For more information on determining feature representations, visit the websites at

- www.pearsoned.ca/text/ogrady/phonology/feat_reps
- www.pearsoned.ca/text/ogrady/phonology/representations
- www.pearsoned.ca/text/ogrady/phonology/feat_hier

FEATURE EXERCISES

1. State the feature that distinguishes each of the following pairs of sounds. (There may be more than one correct answer.) The first is done for you.

    a. [θ] / [ð]   [+/− voice]

    b. [p] / [f]   _____

    c. [s] / [θ]   _____

    d. [b] / [m]   _____

    e. [ʧ] / [ʃ]   _____

2. Each of the following sets contains three sounds which belong to the same natural class. Add one other segment to each set, making sure that the natural class is preserved. Indicate the feature (including its value) which distinguishes the natural class. The first is done for you.

		Segment Added	Distinguishing Feature
a.	[l̩ ə n̩]	[o]	[+ syllabic]
b.	[θ s f]	[ ]	_____
c.	[p m k]	[ ]	_____
d.	[j r n]	[ ]	_____
e.	[ð f s]	[ ]	_____

3. Name the natural class which each of the following phonetic matrices describe.

    a. $\begin{bmatrix} - \text{consonantal} \\ - \text{syllabic} \end{bmatrix}$

    b. $\begin{bmatrix} +\text{consonantal} \\ -\text{syllabic} \\ -\text{sonorant} \\ +\text{continuant} \\ +\text{voice} \end{bmatrix}$

4. In each of the sets below, all the sounds except one constitute a natural class. Draw a circle around the sound which does not belong and state the feature which the remaining sounds share.

   a. [t g v dʒ] _____

   b. [j m ʒ w] _____

   c. [m g d r] _____

   d. [tʃ m t ŋ] _____

5. In each consonant system below, some segments are boxed. Determine if the boxed segments constitute a natural class. If they do, then state the feature(s) that make them a

   a.
   ```
   p    t    k
   f    s
   m    n    ŋ
        l
   w         j
   ```

   b.
   ```
   p    t         k
   b
        s    ʃ        h
        r
   ```

   c.
   ```
   p    t    k
   v    z
   m̩    n̩
        l̩
              i    u
                   a
   ```

   d.
   ```
   p    t    k
   b    d    g
   m    n    ŋ
        l
   ```

   natural class.

6. Provide a feature matrix for each of the following sounds.

   a. [ð θ f v]   c. [u o]

   b. [g dʒ]   d. [i ɪ e ɛ æ]

RULES AND STATEMENTS

To understand and be able to put together rules and statements whenever your analysis uncovers allophones of the same phoneme, you need to remember that....

⇒ Allophones of the same phoneme are in complementary distribution. Rules and statements capture the distribution of the allophones. Rules and statements convey the same information, the difference being that rules use phonological notation, while statements use articulatory descriptions. Since sound changes usually affect classes of sounds rather than individual sounds, we try and make our rules and statements as general as possible.

⇒ Allophones of the same phoneme represent a predictable sound change. Such sound changes occur because segments are often affected by the phonetic characteristics of neighboring sounds. These changes are described using articulatory processes such as assimilation. Rules and statements, therefore, are also descriptions of these articulatory processes.

Rules and statements have three parts:

1. the phoneme
2. the allophone (what the change is)
3. the phonetic environment (where the change occurs)

Convert these statements into rules. Watch out for natural classes!

1. Voiced oral stops become voiceless at the beginning of words.

   _____

2. Alveopalatal affricates become fricatives between vowels.

   _____

3. Vowels become nasalized before nasals.

   _____

4. Schwa is deleted word finally.

   _____

5. A schwa is inserted between a voiceless bilabial stop and a voiced lateral liquid.

   _____

Convert the following rules into statements. Make your statements as general as possible.

1. t -----> $t^ʔ$ / ?_____

_____

2. $\left\{\begin{array}{c} f \\ s \\ \theta \\ ʃ \end{array}\right\}$ ----> $\left\{\begin{array}{c} v \\ z \\ ð \\ ʒ \end{array}\right\}$ / V____V

_____

3. $\left\{\begin{array}{c} i \\ e \end{array}\right\}$ ----> $\left\{\begin{array}{c} ɪ \\ ɛ \end{array}\right\}$ / _____#

_____

4. $\left\{\begin{array}{c} p \\ t \\ k \end{array}\right\}$ ----> $\left\{\begin{array}{c} p^h \\ t^h \\ k^h \end{array}\right\}$ / #_____V́

_____

Now ... Go back over the rules (not the statements you constructed) on this page and formulate them using feature matrices rather than phonetic symbols. Do the same for the rules you constructed (not the statements given) on the previous page.

MORE PHONOLOGY PROBLEMS!

For each of the following data sets:

- determine whether the sounds under consideration are allophones of the same phoneme or separate phonemes or whether they are in free variation. Provide evidence to support your conclusion along with a representation of the phoneme.

- If the sounds are allophones of the same phoneme, then provide a phonological rule along with a statement. Try formulating your rules using features.

While the data are from hypothetical languages, they exemplify phenomena found in real languages.

1. Storish: [ʃ] and [ʒ]

1.	[gasaʃ]	mistake	5.	[trutuʃ]	dive
2.	[ʒipaʃ]	head	6.	[tolʒog]	crash
3.	[sesor]	board	7.	[naʒut]	hospital
4.	[tʌʒəkəʃ]	ambulance	8.	[ʧisoʃ]	operation

2. Nonamb: [i] and [ĩ]

1.	[θikig]	weasel	5.	[apĩŋk]	fox
2.	[gorĩm]	parrot	6.	[nuret]	knife
3.	[seyit]	arrow	7.	[ʌlĩnd]	ferret
4.	[kĩŋglɔn]	cave	8.	[kuʧis]	deer

3. Skatik: [p] and [f]

1.	[pʊnt]	scale	5.	[lɔnik]	scone
2.	[akog]	scatter	6.	[jɪptu]	scold
3.	[zifug]	skelter	7.	[fʊnt]	skate
4.	[jɪftu]	scare	8.	[sipək]	skin

4. Severenese: [i] and [u]

1.	[ubren]	table	5.	[ublet]	never
2.	[lezun]	clock	6.	[seti]	blue
3.	[gunob]	arm	7.	[iplet]	stop
4.	[setu]	moss	8.	[ibren]	snow

5. Luru: [u] and [ʊ]

1.	[luska]	stone	8.	[surku]	to run
2.	[holu]	fly	9.	[umʊlo]	they have
3.	[sʊrak]	left	10.	[rukoru]	singing
4.	[ketʊl]	arm	11.	[uzmaluk]	road
5.	[sumbu]	melon	12.	[ketuĵ]	summer
6.	[ambʊl]	yellow	13.	[ʊrkʊl]	spark
7.	[mastuf]	puppy	14.	[mustʊf]	wine

6. Silliese: [t] and [d]

a.	[madan]	joke	e.	[tar]	chip
b.	[tordalu]	club	f.	[bondel]	laugh
c.	[andar]	sneeze	g.	[godu]	funny
d.	[tili]	drink	h.	[toko]	light

7. Breakie: [p] and [b]

a.	[petikt]	juice	e.	[lopibe]	milk
b.	[dob]	sugar	f.	[θupaz]	egg
c.	[fæbe]	table	g.	[bagur]	bread
d.	[sepita]	food	h.	[gitip]	salt

REMINDER! REMINDER!

When you find allophones of the same phoneme, there is a quick way to determine if your solution is in all likelihood correct. If your rule and statement describe an articulatory process such as assimilation, which is the result of neighbouring sounds interacting with each other, then your solution is probably correct. If your rule and statement do not describe such a process, then you might want to re-think your analysis!

DERIVATIONS

Derivations are a representation of how phonemes and allophones are related. Phonetic forms are derived from phonemic forms by applying phonological processes in the form of a rule. There are three parts to a derivation. These parts are very similar to the components of a phonological rule.

⇒ **Underlying Representation (UR).** The underlying representation is a representation of native speaker knowledge and is always in phonemic transcription.

⇒ **Rules.** Remember that phonemes and allophones are linked by a rule. The rule applies to change the phoneme into the allophone. This, of course, only occurs when the structural description (environment) specified in the rule is found in the underlying representation.

⇒ **Phonetic Representation (PR).** The phonetic representation is also called the surface representation. Since the surface representation always represents pronunciation, it is in phonetic transcription.

In English, liquids become voiceless after a voiceless stop at the beginning of a syllable. This is an example of devoicing and can be captured with a rule such as:

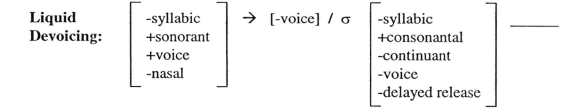

The first feature matrix captures the class of liquids. The second part of the rule captures the change in voicing that occurs. The third part of the rule captures the fact that the process only applies after a voiceless stop at the beginning of a syllable. Recall that σ is used to indicate a syllable.

The following derivation captures the relationship between English voiced and voiceless liquids as shown by the above rule.

UR	# pliz # 'please'	# læf # 'laugh'
Liquid Devoicing	# pl̥iz #	———
PR	[pl̥iz]	[læf]

In the word 'please', Liquid Devoicing applies because [l] occurs after a voiceless consonant (i.e., [p]). The structural description of the rule has been met. Notice that after the rule has applied, [l] has become voiceless (i.e., [l̥]). The rule does not apply to the word 'laugh', as indicated by the dashed line, since the structural description necessary for the rule to apply was not met: [l] occurs at the beginning of the word and not after a voiceless consonant. The phonetic form, therefore, remains the same as the phonemic form.

RULE ORDERING

More than one rule can apply during the derivation of a particular form. Sometimes the order in which rules apply is crucial to deriving the appropriate phonetic form. That is, one rule must apply before another. An example involves the rule of liquid devoicing (from page 65) and the rule of schwa deletion presented below.

Schwa Deletion: $[ə] \rightarrow ø / C_ø \underline{\hspace{2cm}} σ C_ø V$
$$[+stress]$$

The first and second parts of the rule refer to the deletion of schwa. The third part of the rule captures the fact that this occurs only when schwa is in an open syllable followed by a stressed syllable. The first $C_ø$ represents any number of successive onset consonants, from zero up, that may occur before schwa. σ represents the syllable boundary, and the second $C_ø$ again represents any onset consonants that may occur before the stressed vowel of the next syllable.

The Incorrect Order ... Schwa Deletion must apply before Liquid Devoicing. If Liquid Devoicing is applied before schwa deletion, then liquids incorrectly remain voiced in the phonetic form. This is shown in the following derivation of the word 'police'.

UR	# pəlís # 'police'
Liquid Devoicing	————
Schwa Deletion	# plís #
PR	[plís]

(**Note:** It is assumed that stress placement has already occurred. Normally, stress would not be present in the underlying form because it is predictable in English, and therefore would be applied using a stress rule.)

The Correct Order ...   Since liquids in English are produced without voice following a voiceless stop, schwa deletion must occur first so that in the resulting output, liquids occur after voiceless stops, creating the necessary environment for Liquid Devoicing to apply.

UR	# pəlís # 'police'
Schwa Deletion	# plís #
Liquid Devoicing	# pl̥ís #
PR	[pl̥ís]

As shown in the above derivation, the phonetic form now contains, as it should in English, a voiceless liquid!

QUICK REMINDER!

Underlying representations capture the phonological knowledge speakers have about the contrastive sounds of their language. Therefore, these representations are always in phonemic transcription, which does not contain any predictable phonetic information.

Since surface representations capture actual phonetic outputs, they are always in phonetic transcription. That is, they contain all of the predictable phonetic information not found in the underlying representation.

Processes, in the form of rules, apply to add predictable phonetic information to the underlying representation, thereby creating the surface representation!

STILL MORE PHONOLOGY PROBLEMS!!

For each data set:

- determine if the sounds are allophones of the same phoneme, allophones of separate phonemes, or in free variation. Remember to provide evidence in support of your conclusion along with a representation of the phoneme(s).

- for all allophones of the same phoneme, provide a rule and a statement. Wherever possible, try to write one rule and statement for all the sounds you have investigated. HINT ... watch out for natural classes!

- for all allophones of the same phoneme involving natural classes, write a rule using feature notation.

- for all allophones of the same phoneme, identify the articulatory process that your rule describes.

- provide derivations as indicated.

1. <u>Canadian French</u>:   [t] and [ts]

[ts]	This symbol represents a voiceless alveolar affricate
[y]	This symbol represents a high front tense rounded vowel
[ʏ]	This symbol represents a high front lax rounded vowel

1. [ty]	all	7. [telegram]	telegram
2. [abutsi]	ended	8. [trɛ]	very
3. [tɛl]	such	9. [kyltsur]	culture
4. [tab]	stamp	10. [minʏt]	minute
5. [tsimɪd]	timid	11. [tsy]	you
6. [tsɪt]	title	12. [tsʏb]	tube

- provide a derivation for #5, #10, and #12

2. Burmese: [m] and [m̥],   [n] and [n̥],   [ŋ] and [ŋ̥]

Hint: Given that you have been asked to investigate three sets of nasals, would you expect all the nasals to pattern in the same way?

1. [mi]   five   8. [hm̥i]   to lean against
2. [mwej]   to give birth   9. [hm̥wej]   fragrant
3. [mji?]   river   10. [hm̥jaj?]   to cure
4. [ne]   small   11. [hn̥ej]   slow
5. [nwe]   to bend   12. [hn̥a]   to lend property
6. [ŋa]   five   13. [hŋ̥wej]   to heat
7. [ŋou?]   tree stump   14. [hn̥e?]   bird

• provide a derivation for #3, #9, and #13

3. Malay: [t] and [tʲ]

[ʲ]   This diacritic represents a sound that has been palatalized.

1. [tarek]   pull   6. [tʲampah]   tasteless
2. [kətʲut]   shriveled   7. [kətil]   pinch
3. [pitər]   disk   8. [tʲarek]   rip
4. [ʧomel]   cute   9. [lawat]   visit
5. [batʲa]   steel   10. [ʧampah]   tasteless

• Look at the Malay data again and examine [tʲ] and [ʧ]. What conclusion can you make about these two sounds? Give evidence to support your answer.

4. Tamil: [p] and [b],   [k] and [g],   [ṭ] and [ḍ],   [t̪] and [d̪]

[.]   This diacritic means that a sound is retroflex.
[̪]   This diacritic means that a sound is dental.
[ɨ]   This symbol represents a high central unrounded vowel.

Remember: When looking for complementary distribution, you must record the immediate surrounding phonetic environment around EACH OCCURRENCE of a sound.

1.	[pal]	tooth		11.	[id̪ɨ]	this
2.	[abayam]	refuge		12.	[ad̪ɨ]	that
3.	[kappal]	ship		13.	[kaṭṭi]	knife
4.	[saabam]	curse		14.	[kuḍi]	jump
5.	[kaakkaaj]	crow		15.	[paṭṭi]	ten
6.	[mugil]	cloud		16.	[paaḍam]	foot
7.	[t̪ugil]	veil		17.	[iḍam]	place
8.	[t̪aṭṭɨ]	plate		18.	[kaaṭpaaḍi]	name of a town
9.	[padɨ]	lie down		19.	[paṭṭɨ]	silk
10.	[t̪uukkɨ]	carry				

• provide a derivation for #3, #6, and #14

5. Igbirra: [e] and [a]

1.	[mezi]	I expect		5.	[mazɪ]	I am in pain
2.	[meze]	I am well		6.	[mazɛ]	I agree
3.	[meto]	I arrange		7.	[matɔ]	I pick
4.	[metu]	I beat		8.	[matʊ]	I send

• Are there minimal pairs?
• [e] and [a] both occur between m _ z and m _ t. What significance does this have for your analysis?

6. <u>Gascon:</u>   [b] and [β],   [d] and [ð],   [g] and [ɣ]

> Hint: Think about what process you would expect given pairs of stops and fricatives.

> [ɣ]   This symbol represents a voiced velar fricative.

1.	[brẽn]	endanger	10.	[ʒuɣɛt]	he played
2.	[dilys]	Monday	11.	[krãmbo]	room
3.	[taldepãn]	leftover bread	12.	[eʃaðo]	hoe
4.	[ʃiβaw]	horse	13.	[gat]	cat
5.	[pũnde]	to lay eggs	14.	[aβe]	to have
6.	[agro]	sour	15.	[biɣar]	mosquito
7.	[puðe]	to be able	16.	[ũmbro]	shadow
8.	[riɣut]	he laughed	17.	[dudze]	twelve
9.	[noβi]	husband	18.	[lũŋg]	long

- Examine the Gascon data again, paying attention to the oral and nasal vowels. Can you make any conclusions about nasalized vowels in this language? Write one statement involving classes of sounds, describing their behavior.

- Provide a derivation for #3, #9, #12, and #16. Do your rules need to be ordered? Why or why not?

REMINDER ... REMINDER ...

To solve a phonology problem, you must have a firm grasp on minimal pairs, near minimal pairs, complementary distribution, phonemes, and allophones. If you don't, then you need to get some help!

REVIEW! REVIEW!   Make sure you can:

- — define phonemes and allophones
- — spot minimal and near minimal pairs
- — find free variation
- — determine complementary distribution
- — construct representations of phonemes
- — construct syllable representations
- — spot open and closed syllables
- — identify consonantal and vowel features
- — put together feature matrices
- — put together rules and statements
- — put together rules using feature notation
- — construct derivations
- — solve phonology problems

QUESTIONS? PROBLEMS? DIFFICULTIES?

_____

_____

_____

_____

_____

_____

_____

_____

_____

_____

_____

_____

CHAPTER 4. MORPHOLOGY: THE ANALYSIS OF WORD STRUCTURE

Morphology is the study of words and how they are formed and interpreted. Some of the important topics and concepts found in this chapter include:

1. morphological terminology
2. identifying morphemes
3. identifying lexical categories
4. analyzing word structure
5. derivation
6. compounding
7. inflection
8. other morphological phenomena
9. morphology problems
10. morphophonemics

MORPHOLOGICAL TERMINOLOGY

The following terms are crucial to understanding morphology. You should know them!

TERM	DEFINITION
Word	Words are the smallest free-forms found in language. Free-forms are elements which can appear in isolation, or whose position is not fixed. Words can be simple or complex.
Morpheme	A morpheme is the smallest meaning or functional unit found in language. Morphemes can be free or bound.
Allomorphs	Allomorphs are the different forms of a morpheme.
Affixes	Affixes are different types of bound morphemes. There are three types of affixes found in language: prefixes, suffixes, and infixes.
Root	A root is the core of a word. It is the portion of the word that carries most of the word's meaning.
Base	A base is any form to which an affix is added.
Stem	A stem is a base to which an inflectional affix is added.

IDENTIFYING MORPHEMES

Morphemes are the building blocks of words. A word may contain only one morpheme, making it a simple word, or a word may contain more than one morpheme, making it a complex word. Below are some hints for determining the number of morphemes that a word contains.

⇒ A morpheme carries information about meaning or function. For example, the word 'haunt' cannot be divided into the morphemes 'h' and 'aunt', since only 'aunt' has meaning. However, the word 'bats' has two morphemes, since both 'bat' and 's' have meaning. The 's', of course, means that there is more than one.

⇒ The meanings of individual morphemes should contribute to the overall meaning of the word. For example, 'pumpkin' cannot be divided into 'pump' and 'kin' since the meaning of 'pumpkin' has nothing to do with the meaning of either 'pump' or 'kin'.

⇒ A morpheme is not the same as a syllable. Morphemes do not have to be a syllable. Morphemes can consist of one or more syllables. For example, the morpheme 'treat' has one syllable, the morpheme 'dracula' has three syllables, but the morpheme 's' meaning plural is not a syllable.

⇒ Often as words are built, changes in pronunciation and/or spelling occur. These do not affect a morpheme's status as a morpheme. For example, when 'y' is attached to the morpheme 'scare', it becomes 'scary', and when 'er' is attached to 'scary', it becomes 'scarier'. The root for both 'scary' and 'scarier' is 'scare' and not 'scar', and the base for 'scarier' is 'scary'.

Identify the number of morphemes in each of the following words.

insert	_____	supply	_____
memory	_____	supplies	_____
		supplier	_____
format	_____	faster	_____
flowchart	_____	power	_____
bug	_____	processor	_____
debug	_____		

MORPHEMES! MORPHEMES!

For each of the following words, identify the number of morphemes and write the free and bound morphemes in the appropriate blanks. A free morpheme can be a word by itself, while a bound morpheme must be attached to another element. Remember, a word may have more than one bound morpheme. The first is done for you.

WORD	TOTAL # OF MORPHEMES	FREE	BOUND
eraser	2	erase	-er
wicked			
invalid (A)			
invalid (N)			
Jack's			
optionality			
refurnish			
inabilities			
denationalize			
present			
activation			

IDENTIFYING LEXICAL CATEGORIES

In morphology, we are concerned with four lexical categories: nouns, verbs, adjectives, and prepositions. Nouns typically refer to concrete and abstract things. Verbs typically denote actions. Adjectives usually name properties. Prepositions generally encode spatial relations.

For each of the words below, state the number of morphemes found in the word, and identify the root, the lexical category of the root, and the lexical category of the entire word. Remember, the root is the core of the word and carries most of the word's meaning. Be careful: the root's lexical category and the word's lexical category may or may not be the same. The first is done for you.

WORD	# OF MORPHS	ROOT	ROOT CATEGORY	WORD CATEGORY
kindnesses	3	kind	adjective	noun
amazement				
reusable				
dishonest				
Calgary				
lovelier				
historical				
uncontrolled				
impersonal				
trees				
faster				
rereads				
beautiful				
child				

WORD STRUCTURE

A word tree is a representation of a word's internal structure. To put together a word tree you need to be able to determine the number of morphemes in a word, identify roots and affixes, and assign lexical categories. Remember, prefixes are attached to the front of a base, while suffixes are attached to the end of a base. Infixes are a type of affix that occurs inside another morpheme. Infixes are not found in English.

Below are some examples of how to draw a word tree.

1. Words with a single affix.

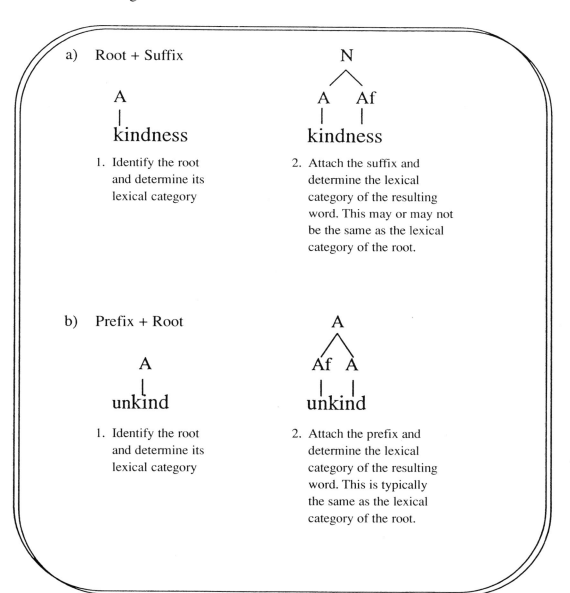

a)   Root + Suffix

A
|
kindness

1. Identify the root and determine its lexical category

N
／＼
A   Af
| |
kindness

2. Attach the suffix and determine the lexical category of the resulting word. This may or may not be the same as the lexical category of the root.

b)   Prefix + Root

A
|
unkind

1. Identify the root and determine its lexical category

A
／＼
Af   A
| |
unkind

2. Attach the prefix and determine the lexical category of the resulting word. This is typically the same as the lexical category of the root.

2.   Words with multiple suffixes.

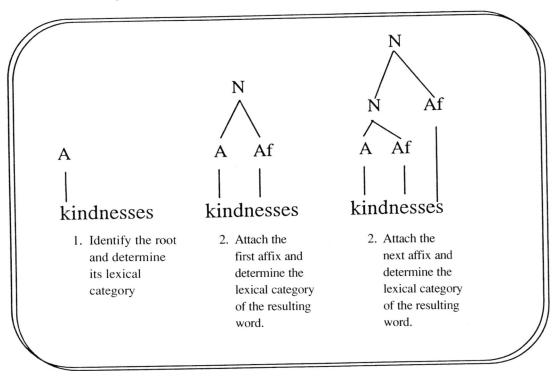

3.   Words with both a prefix and a suffix.

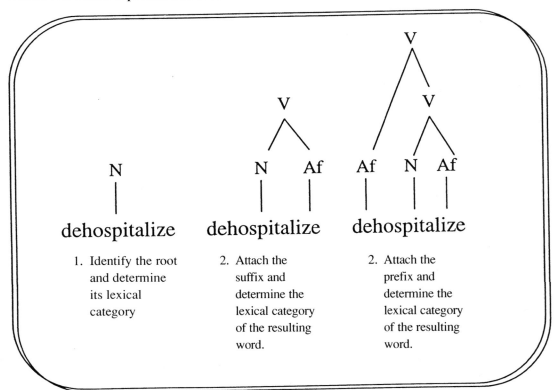

4.   Words that are structurally ambiguous.

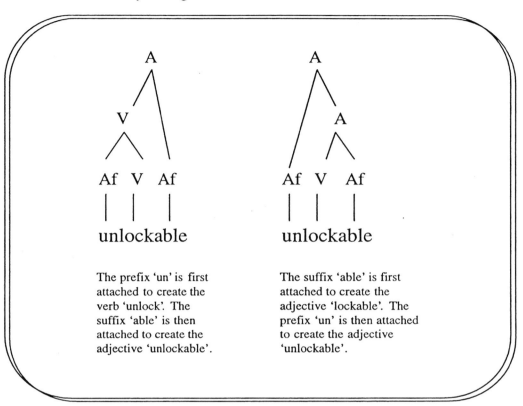

The prefix 'un' is first attached to create the verb 'unlock'. The suffix 'able' is then attached to create the adjective 'unlockable'.

The suffix 'able' is first attached to create the adjective 'lockable'. The prefix 'un' is then attached to create the adjective 'unlockable'.

Exercise! Exercise! To practice, draw trees for the following words:

- trees
- lovelier
- dishonest
- beautiful

- amazement
- reusable
- impersonal
- Calgary

REMINDER! REMINDER!

To be able to draw word trees correctly, you need to be able to identify nouns, verbs, adjectives, and prepositions. If you are having difficulty with these, get some help!

DERIVATION

Derivation is a process of affixation. Affixation is a morphological process which adds affixes to words. Derivational affixes are affixes which:

- build a word having a different (but usually related) semantic content than that of its base,
- usually change the lexical category of a word,
- occur closer to the root than do inflectional affixes, and which
- are less productive, meaning there are restrictions on the class of bases to which they can attach.

English has many derivational affixes. English derivational suffixes have all of the characteristics of derivation just described. For example:

- -ity combines with an adjective such as 'stupid' to create the noun 'stupidity', meaning the result of being 'stupid'.
- -ful combines with a noun such as 'faith' to create the adjective 'faithful', meaning having 'faith'.
- -ment combines with a verb such as 'adjourn' to create the noun 'adjournment', meaning the result of 'adjourning'.

English also has many derivational prefixes; however, these do not change the lexical category of the base. Despite this, English prefixes are still considered derivational. This is because of the semantic change that occurs when they are used to build words. For example:

- re- combines with a verb such as 'do' to create the verb 'redo', meaning to do again.
- anti- combines with a noun such as 'abortion' to create the noun 'anti-abortion', meaning against abortion.

For more examples of English derivational prefixes and suffixes, see Table 4.6 on page 105 in the textbook.

Derivational affixes are often subject to restrictions. For example:

- Derivational affixes combine with bases of particular lexical categories.

  e.g.,   -ize must be attached to a noun / -er must be attached to a verb
- Derivational affixes combine with bases having certain phonological properties.

  e.g.,   -en must be attached to a base having one syllable and ending in an obstruent
- Derivational affixes combine with bases of specific origin.

  e.g.,   -ant must be attached to a base of Latin origin

Try this!   Draw trees for the following words. Remember that a word can contain more than one derivational affix.

- disappear
- homeless
- electricity

- unbreakable
- instituitional
- lodger

Now... go back over the above words and identify which affixes are Class I affixes and which belong to Class II. Remember, Class I affixes often cause a phonological change to the base, but Class II affixes do not!

COMPOUNDING

Compounding is another technique for building words. Compounding involves the combination of two or more already existing words into a new word. There are four important properties of English compounds:

⇒ **Headedness.** The head of a compound is the morpheme that determines the category of the entire compound. Most English compounds are right-headed. That is, the category of the entire compound is the same as the category of the rightmost member of the compound. Most English compounds are nouns, verbs, and adjectives. For example, since the rightmost member *board* is a noun, the compound *blackboard* is a noun.

⇒ **Stress Patterns.** Even though compounds can be spelled as one word, two words, or with a hyphen separating the morphemes, a generalization can be made about the stress patterns found on them. Stress tends to be more prominent on the first member of the compound rather than the second: for example, *greénhouse* (a garden centre) versus *green hoúse* (a house that is green).

⇒ **Tense/Plural.** Tense and plural markers are usually added to the compound as a whole and not to the first member of the compound. For example, the plural of *fire engine* is *fire engines* and not *fires engine*. Similarly, the past tense of *drop kick* is *drop kicked* and not *dropped kick*.

⇒ **Semantic Patterns.** Compounds are used to express a wide range of meaning relationships. Many compounds are endocentric. In an endocentric compound, the entire compound denotes a subtype of the head. For example, a *tea-cup* is a type of *cup*, and a *lunch-room* is a type of *room*. Some compounds are exocentric. In an exocentric compound, the meaning of the compound does not come from the head. For example, a *redneck* is not a type of *neck*, but a type of person.

Another type of compounding is called incorporation. Incorporation usually involves combining nouns with a verb to form a compound verb.

e.g.,   Without Incorporation: They are <u>cleaning</u> the <u>house</u>.

      With Incorporation: They are <u>housecleaning</u>.

Incorporation is not very common in English, but can be found in many languages.

Compounding can be used in conjunction with derivation to build words. Draw trees for each of the following words.

- washer-dryer
- presidential election
- (an) undertaking
- baby blue

EXERCISE!

For each compound below, state the lexical categories making it up and give another example of that type of compound. The first is done for you.

COMPOUND	LEXICAL CATEGORIES	EXAMPLE
bathroom	Noun + Noun	movie star
scarecrow	_____	_____
skin-deep	_____	_____
bittersweet	_____	_____
upstairs	_____	_____

Now go back and draw a word tree for each compound!

INFLECTION

Inflection involves modifying the form of a word to indicate grammatical information such as singular versus plural or past versus non-past.

Inflection is most commonly a process of affixation. Affixation adds affixes to words. Inflectional affixes are affixes which:

- function to provide grammatical information,
- never change the lexical category of a word,
- occur after derivational affixes, and which are
- productive, meaning there are relatively few exceptions.

English only has eight inflectional affixes. For example:

ON NOUNS:

- -s can be added to a noun such as 'dog' to indicate the plural, as in 'There are six dog<u>s</u>.'
- -'s can be added to a noun such as 'dog' to indicate the possessive, as in 'The dog<u>'s</u> bone is on the floor."

ON VERBS:

- -s can be added to a verb such as 'walk' to indicate the 3rd person singular present tense, as in 'He walk<u>s</u> slowly."
- -ed can be added to a verb such as 'walk' to indicate the past tense, as in 'He walk<u>ed</u> slowly."
- -ing can be added to a verb such as 'walk' to indicate that the action is still in progress, as in 'He is walk<u>ing</u> slowly."
- -en or -ed can be added to a verb such as 'eat' or 'walk' to indicate that an action is complete, as in 'He has eat<u>en</u>' or 'He has walk<u>ed</u> home."

ON ADJECTIVES:

- -er can be added to an adjective such as 'tall' to indicate the comparative, as in 'John is tall<u>er</u> than Mary.'
- -est can be added to an adjective such as 'tall' to indicate the superlative, as in 'John is the tall<u>est</u> in his family.'

PRACTICE! For each of the following words, identify the lexical category of the root and the type of inflectional information found (i.e., past tense, superlative, plural, etc.). The first is done for you.

WORD	LEXICAL CATEGORY	INFLECTIONAL INFORMATION
1. watched	verb	past tense
2. runs	_____	_____
3. sorriest	_____	_____
4. lamps	_____	_____
5. playing	_____	_____
6. driven	_____	_____
7. lovelier	_____	_____

IDENTIFY THE AFFIX

For each of the following English words, state whether it is simple or complex. If it is complex, state whether the affix is inflectional or derivational. The first is done for you.

WORD	SIMPLE / COMPLEX	INFL / DERIV
desks	Complex	Inflectional
fly	_____	_____
prettier	_____	_____
stringy	_____	_____
delight	_____	_____
reuse	_____	_____
fastest	_____	_____
mistreat	_____	_____

MORE ON INFLECTION

In addition to affixation, inflection can also be marked using internal change, suppletion, reduplication and tone placement.

PROCESS	DEFINITION
Internal Change	This process provides grammatical information by changing a portion of the morpheme. That is, the tense or number of a word is marked by replacing a segment within the morpheme for another. e.g., r<u>u</u>n → r<u>a</u>n
Suppletion	This process provides grammatical information by changing the entire morpheme. That is, the tense, number, etc. of a word is marked by replacing one morpheme with an entirely different morpheme. e.g., go → went Partial suppletion is sometimes used to describe the change in words such as think → thought in which more than a segment has been changed, but not the entire morpheme.
Reduplication	A process which copies all (full) or a portion (partial) of the base to mark a semantic or grammatical contrast. This process is not productive in English. e.g., Turkish: iyi 'well' → iyi iyi 'very well' Tagalog: lakad 'walk' → lalakad 'will walk'
Tone Placement	This process is similar to stress placement in that a difference in tone can be used to create different words, or to mark a change in tense or number. This process is found in tone languages. e.g., Mono Bili: Past (High Tone) Future (Low Tone) dá 'spanked dà 'will spank' wó 'killed' wò 'will kill'

Exercise! Exercise!   Each of the following words has been inflected. For each, identify the type of inflectional process that has been used to mark the grammatical contrast. The first has been done for you.

WORD	TYPE OF INFLECTION
drove	internal change
was	
(is) jumping	
anak anak 'all sorts of children'	
better	
lovelier	
George's	
tatakbuh 'will run'	
mice	

REMINDER!

Many more inflectional phenomena, including case and agreement, are widely used in language. For more information on these, visit

www.pearsoned.ca/text/ogrady/morphology/inflection AND
www.pearsoned.ca/text/ogrady/syntax/case

FORM VS. FUNCTION

Many affixes have the same form, but different functions. That is, affixes having the same form can be either inflectional or derivational, or they can be different inflectional or derivational affixes. You need to be able to identify affixes according to their function rather than their form. The following exercise should help!

In each group of four words below, two words have the same type of affix, one word has a different affix, and one word has no affix at all. Next to each word, write S (same), D (different) or N (none) based on the items in the set. You may want to use a dictionary. The first is done for you.

1. ovens   __S__
      lens   __N__
      hens   __S__
      listens   __D__

2. greener   _____
      farmer   _____
      colder   _____
      water   _____

3. greedy   _____
      ivory   _____
      jealousy   _____
      dirty   _____

4. friendly   _____
      slowly   _____
      intelligently   _____
      early   _____

5. leaven   _____
      harden   _____
      spoken   _____
      thicken   _____

6. intelligent   _____
      inhale   _____
      incongruous   _____
      inhuman   _____

7. rider   _____
      colder   _____
      silver   _____
      actor   _____

8. candied   _____
      shopped   _____
      cleaned   _____
      candid   _____

MORE PRACTICE WITH WORD TREES

Draw one tree for each of the words listed below and identify whether inflection, derivation, and/or compounding was used to build the word. Remember that more than one process can be used in a single word. Use the context sentence to help you determine the lexical category of the entire word!

For example, the tree for the word 'workable', as in the sentence ***I like the <u>workable</u> solution,*** might be diagrammed as follows:

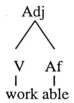   Derivation

WORD	CONTEXT SENTENCE
1. taken	The baby has <u>taken</u> his first steps.
2. spoonfeeding	Mother is <u>spoonfeeding</u> the baby.
3. softest	The <u>softest</u> pillow has the
4. silkiest	<u>silkiest</u> cover.
5. introductions	Mary performed the <u>introductions</u>.
6. steps	John <u>steps</u> up the ladder.
7. steps	I hate those steep <u>steps</u>.
8. stringier	My hair is <u>stringier</u> than hers.
9. skiers	The <u>skiers</u> were rich.
10. father	My <u>father</u> lives in France.
11. stone-cold	Your french-fries are <u>stone-cold</u>.
12. making	Jill is <u>making</u> candy.
13. boxing	We watched the <u>boxing</u>.
14. criticize	You <u>criticize</u> too much.

15. creamy   Creamy chocolate is delicious.

16. keepers   The keepers locked up.

17. blessing   Give me your blessing.

18. blessing   She is blessing the bread.

19. school teacher   My mother was a school teacher.

20. clumsiness   I detest clumsiness.

21. windmills   Holland has lots of windmills.

22. hammered   John hammered on the door.

23. thickeners   There are many different types of thickeners.

24. unlocked   We unlocked the door.

25. declaw   You should declaw your cat.

26. retry   She should retry the recipe.

27. inside   The cat is inside the box.

28. impure   Impure water is dangerous.

29. sleepwalking   George is often found sleepwalking.

30. defrosting   The steaks are defrosting.

QUICK REMINDER!

Remember that ALL English prefixes are derivational even though they do not cause a lexical category change!

OTHER MORPHOLOGICAL PHENOMENA

PROCESS	DEFINITION
Cliticization	Clitics are morphemes that behave like words in terms of meaning and function. Clitics differ, though, in that they cannot stand alone as a word. Cliticization attaches these elements to either the beginning of a following word or the end of a preceding word. e.g., 're' from 'are' is attached to 'they' as in they're
Conversion	A process which assigns an existing word to a different lexical category. e.g., butter (N) → (to) butter (V)
Clipping	A process which shortens a polysyllabic word by removing one or more syllables. e.g., condominium → condo
Blends	A process which creates a new word by combining non-morphemic portions of two existing words. e.g., spiced + ham → spam
Backformation	A process which creates a word by removing a supposed affix from an existing word. e.g., enthuse ← enthusiasm
Acronyms	A process which creates new words using the initial letters of the words in a phrase or title. e.g., scuba, Unicef
Onomatopoeia	Words that have been created to sound like the thing they name. e.g., buzz, hiss, sizzle
Coinage	A process which creates a totally new word. e.g., Teflon New words can also be created from names. e.g., boycott

Practice! Practice! Identify the process responsible for formation of each of the following English words. Choose any of the morphological phenomena from the above table as well as inflection, derivation, and compounding. The first is done for you.

1. infomercial   blending _____

2. (to) ship   _____

3. mice   _____

4. support-hose   _____

5. chirp   _____

6. jumped   _____

7. healthy   _____

8. demo   _____

9. sadness   _____

10. he's   _____

11. head-line   _____

12. beep   _____

13. ATM   _____

There are many examples of different word formation processes in the following passage. Find all the examples of ACRONYM, BACKFORMATION, BLENDING, CLIPPING, COINAGE, and COMPOUNDING.

> John didn't enthuse about UCLA, as he probably expected his profs to spoon feed him. He preferred to avoid the smog by taking sandwiches to the beach where he would laze around and go scuba diving in his new dacron dry suit. One day he was suffering from a headache and dizziness, which he thought might be caused by sunstroke or the flu, so he went to the doctor. The doc sent him to the lab for a urinalysis and a blood test and suggested that he should see an ENT specialist as well. He is now OK, having returned from the USA, and he is learning about ohms, watts, and volts at MIT.

Get ready for morphology problems ...

INTRODUCTION TO MORPHOLOGY PROBLEMS

The goal in morphology problems is to isolate and identify all the morphemes in the data given. To do this, you must identify recurring strings of sounds and match them with recurring meanings. It sounds harder than it really is. Here are a few easy ones to try!

All data is given in phonetic transcription.

1. Mende (Sierra Leone)

1.	[pɛlɛ]	house	9.	[pɛlɛi]	the house
2.	[mɔm]	glass	10.	[mɔmi]	the glass
3.	[dɔmi]	story	11.	[dɔmii]	the story
4.	[kali]	hoe	12.	[kalii]	the hoe
5.	[hele]	elephant	13.	[helei]	the elephant
6.	[kaamɔ]	teacher	14.	[kaamɔi]	the teacher
7.	[navo]	boy	15.	[navoi]	the boy
8.	[numu]	person	16.	[numui]	the person

a. What is the morpheme meaning 'the'?

b. Given [sale] meaning 'proverb', what is the form for 'the proverb'?

c. If [kpindii] means 'the night', then what does [kpindi] mean?

2. Ganada (Uganda)

1.	[omukazi]	woman	6.	[abakazi]	women
2.	[omusawo]	doctor	7.	[abasawo]	doctors
3.	[omusika]	heir	8.	[abasika]	heirs
4.	[omuwala]	girl	9.	[abawala]	girls
5.	[omulenzi]	boy	10.	[abalenzi]	boys

a. What is the morpheme meaning 'singular'?

b. What is the morpheme meaning 'plural'?

c. Given [abalanga] meaning 'twins', what would the form be for 'twin'?

3. Kanuri (Nigeria)

1.	[gana]	small	6. [nəmgana]	smallness
2.	[kura]	big	7. [nəmkura]	bigness
3.	[kurugu]	long	8. [nəmkurugu]	length
4.	[karite]	excellent	9. [nəmkarite]	excellence
5.	[dibi]	bad	10. [nəmdibi]	badness

a. What type of affix is shown (i.e., prefix, suffix, infix)?

b. What is the affix?

c. Given [kəji] meaning 'sweet', what is the form for 'sweetness'?

d. Given [nəmgəla] meaning 'goodness', what is the form for 'good'?

e. What morphological process was used to form the words in the second column?

f. Draw a word-tree for [nəmkurugu] 'length'.

MORE MORPHOLOGY PROBLEMS

The following pages contain a number of data sets from different languages. These data sets are intended to give you practice in doing morphological analysis. Each contains sufficient data to make valid conclusions; however, the data may have been regularized somewhat. All data is in phonetic transcription.

1. Turkish:

1.	[deniz]	an ocean	9.	[elim]	my hand
2.	[denize]	to an ocean	10.	[eller]	hands
3.	[denizin]	of an ocean	11.	[disler]	teeth
4.	[eve]	to a house	12.	[disimizin]	of our tooth
5.	[evden]	from a house	13.	[dislerimizin]	of our teeth
6.	[evcikden]	from a little house	14.	[elcike]	to a little hand
7.	[denizcikde]	in a little ocean	15.	[denizlerimizde]	in our oceans
8.	[elde]	in a hand	16.	[evciklerimizde]	in our little houses

Give the Turkish morpheme which corresponds to each of the following English translations.

ocean _____   my _____

house _____   our _____

hand _____   of _____

tooth _____   little _____

plural _____   from _____

to _____   in _____

What is the order of morphemes in a Turkish word in terms of noun, preposition, plural, possessive determiner and adjective? (Don't assume that this order will be the same as it is in English!)

What would be the Turkish word meaning 'of our little hands'? (HINT: use the order you determined above.)

2. Bontoc (Philippines)

1.	[fikas]	strong	5.	[fumikas]	he is becoming strong
2.	[kilad]	red	6.	[kumilad]	he is becoming red
3.	[bato]	stone	7.	[bumato]	he is becoming stone
4.	[fusul]	enemy	8.	[fumusul]	he is becoming an enemy

What is the affix used to form the verbs?

What type of affix (i.e., prefix, suffix, infix) is used to form the verbs?

What morphological process is used to build the verbs?

3. Michoacan Aztec (also known as Nahuatl—Mexico)

1.	[nokali]	my house	8.	[mopelo]	your dog
2.	[nokalimes]	my houses	9.	[mopelomes]	your dogs
3.	[mokali]	your house	10.	[ipelo]	his dog
4.	[ikali]	his house	11.	[nokwahmili]	my cornfield
5.	[kali]	house	12.	[mokwahmili]	your cornfield
6.	[kalimes]	houses	13.	[ikwahmili]	his cornfield
7.	[nopelo]	my dog	14.	[ikwahmilimes]	his cornfields

Fill in the blanks with the corresponding Michoacan morphemes:

house _____   my _____

dog _____   your _____

cornfield _____   his _____

plural _____

What does [ipelo] mean in this language?

What would be the form for 'my cornfields' in this language? For 'his dogs'?

4. Isleta (a dialect of Southern Tiwa—New Mexico, U.S.A.)

1. [temiban]   I went   4. [mimiay]   he was going
2. [amiban]   you went   5. [tewanban] I came
3. [temiwe]   I am going   6. [tewanhi]   I will come

List the morphemes corresponding to the following English translations:

I	_____	present progressive	_____
you	_____	past progressive	_____
he	_____	past	_____
go	_____	future	_____
come	_____		

What type of affixes are the subject morphemes?

What type of affixes are the tense morphemes?

What is the order of morphemes in this language?

How would you say the following in this language?

he went   _____

I will go   _____

you were coming _____

5. Isthmus Zapoteco (Mexico)   Note: [ñ] is a palatal nasal

1.	[ñee]	foot	12.	[kazigidu]	our chins
2.	[kañee]	feet	13.	[zike]	shoulder
3.	[ñeebe]	his foot	14.	[zikebe]	his shoulder
4.	[kañeebe]	his feet	15.	[kazikeluʔ]	your shoulders
5.	[ñeeluʔ]	your foot	16.	[diaga]	ear
6.	[kañeetu]	your (pl) feet	17.	[kadiagatu]	your (pl) ears
7.	[kañeedu]	our feet	18.	[kadiagadu]	our ears
8.	[kazigi]	chins	19.	[bisozedu]	our father
9.	[zigibe]	his chin	20.	[bisozetu]	your (pl) father
10.	[zigiluʔ]	your chin	21.	[kabisozetu]	your (pl) fathers
11.	[kazigitu]	your (pl) chins			

List the morphemes of Isthmus Zapoteco which correspond to each of the following words:

foot   _____   your   _____

shoulder   _____   our   _____

father   _____   his   _____

chin   _____   plural   _____

ear   _____

your (pl)   _____

What is the order of morphemes in Isthmus Zapoteco in terms of nouns, possessive determiners and plural?

TWO REMINDERS:

1. An affix is an infix only when it is inserted inside a morpheme.
2. Don't forget to use morphological boundary markers (i.e., dashes) for all bound affixes (prefixes, suffixes, and affixes). Root words do not need morphological boundaries.

6. Fore (Papua New Guinea)

1. [natuwi]	I ate yesterday	8. [natuni]	We ate yesterday
2. [nagasuwi]	I ate today.	9. [nagasuni]	We ate today.
3. [nakuwi]	I will eat.	10. [nagasusi]	We (dual) ate today.
4. [nata:ni]	You ate yesterday.	11. [nakuni]	We will eat.
5. [nata:naw]	You ate yesterday?	12. [nakusi]	We (dual) will eat.
6. [nakiyi]	He will eat.	13. [nata:wi]	They ate yesterday.
7. [nakiyaw]	He will eat?	14. [nata:si]	They (dual) ate yesterday.

- Don't forget that what are inflectional affixes in many languages can be translated into separate words in English.

- 'yesterday', 'today', and 'tomorrow' are translations of the English past, present, and future tenses (respectively).

Identify the Fore morphemes that correspond to the following English words:

I _____	eat _____
he _____	yesterday _____
we _____	today _____
they _____	will _____
we (dual) _____	question _____
they (dual) _____	statement _____

Describe the order of the morphemes in terms of personal pronouns, question/statement markers, verbs, and adverbs.

Give the Fore words for the following:

He ate yesterday? _____

They (dual) will eat? _____

They ate today. _____

MORPHOPHONEMICS

Morphemes do not always have the same form. Allomorphs are the different forms of a morpheme. Consider the following English example.

⇒ **The Allomorphs ...** The English plural morpheme -s has three different phonetic forms:

> [-s] in words like 'cats',
> [-z] in words like 'dogs', and
> [-əz] in words like 'dishes'.

⇒ **The Conditioning Environment ...** Which phonetic form is realized depends on the phonological characteristics of the final segment in the preceding word:

> [-s] occurs after a base ending in a voiceless consonant that is not strident;
> [-z] occurs after a base ending in a voiced consonant that is not strident;
> [-əz] occurs after a base ending in a strident consonant.

The specific environment in which the different allomorphs occur is often referred to as the distribution of the allomorphs. This interaction between morphology and phonology is called **morphophonemics**.

For more information on morphophonemics, visit www.pearsoned.ca/text/ogrady/ morphology/morphophonemics.

Practice! Find the allomorphs in the following data from Luiseno.

Luiseño (Southern California)

1.	[nokaamay]	my son	13.	[pokaamay]	his son
2.	[ʔoki]	your house	14.	[poki]	his house
3.	[potaanat]	his blanket	15.	[notaanat]	my blanket
4.	[ʔohuukapi]	your pipe	16.	[pohuukapi]	his pipe
5.	[ʔotaanat]	your blanket	17.	[nohuukapi]	my pipe
6.	[noki]	my house	18.	[ʔokaamay]	your son
7.	[ʔokim]	your houses	19.	[pompeewum]	their wives
8.	[nokaamayum]	my sons	20.	[camhuukapim]	our pipes
9.	[popeew]	his wife	21.	[ʔotaanatum]	your blankets
10.	[ʔopeew]	your wife	22.	[pomkaamay]	their son
11.	[camtaanat]	our blanket	23.	[campeewum]	our wives
12.	[camhuukapi]	our pipe	24.	[pomkim]	their houses

List the Luiseño morphemes that correspond to the following English words:

son   _____   my   _____

house   _____   his   _____

blanket   _____   your   _____

wife   _____   their   _____

pipe   _____   our   _____

What are the two allomorphs of the Luiseño plural marker?

_____

State the environment in which each of the allomorphs occurs. Be general!

a. _____

b. _____

REVIEW! REVIEW!   Make sure you know how to:

    –   define morphological terms
    –   divide a word into its morphemes
    –   assign lexical categories
    –   build word trees
    –   identify inflection and derivation
    –   construct compound words
    –   recognize endocentric and exocentric compounds
    –   recognize processes used to build words
    –   do morphological analysis
    –   identify morphological processes in unfamiliar languages
    –   find allomorphs

QUESTIONS? PROBLEMS? DIFFICULTIES?

CHAPTER 5. SYNTAX:
THE ANALYSIS OF SENTENCE STRUCTURE

Syntax is the study of the operations that combine words, stored in a speaker's mental lexicon (dictionary), into sentences. Some of the important topics and concepts found in this chapter include:

1. lexical and non-lexical categories phrases
2. phrases
3. phrase structure tests
4. sentences
5. complement clauses
6. complement options
7. merge and move
8. deep and surface structure
9. yes/no and wh-questions
10. inversion and wh-movement
11. verb-raising and do-insertion
12. coordination, relative clauses, and passives

SYNTACTIC CATEGORIES

There are two types of syntactic categories: lexical and non-lexical. Some of the major characteristics of each include:

Lexical:
- words that have meaning
- words that can be inflected
- includes nouns, verbs, adjectives, prepositions, and adverbs

Non-Lexical:
- words whose meaning is harder to define
- words that have a grammatical function
- includes determiners, auxiliary verbs, degree words, and conjunctions

The lexical category to which a word belongs can be determined by examining (1) its meaning, (2) the type of inflectional affixes that it can take, and (3) the non-lexical category words with which it can co-occur.

Be careful! Some words can belong to more than one category.

PRACTICE WITH SYNTACTIC CATEGORIES

Each sentence below has some words underlined in it. Identify the category of each underlined word. Note that the underlined word can be either lexical or non-lexical.

Remember, words can often be assigned to more than one category, so pay close attention to how the word is being used in the sentence!

1. Pamela's heart <u>beat</u> fast <u>and</u> her hands trembled a lot as <u>she</u> listened <u>to</u> the intermittent knocking on <u>the</u> front <u>door</u> of her shanty <u>located</u> near the railroad tracks beside a <u>hobo</u> <u>jungle</u> and she thought, "That's a <u>bum</u> rap, if ever I <u>heard</u> one."

2. The <u>railroad</u> <u>agent</u> told the <u>Navajo</u>, "The <u>coming</u> of the Iron Horse <u>will</u> <u>bring</u> great prosperity to <u>the</u> Redman," but the Indians <u>had</u> <u>reservations</u>.

3. "The <u>leg</u>, he is fractured," he <u>said</u> <u>in</u> broken English.

4. The Great Barrier Reef is 900 miles long <u>and</u> Wilmer Chanti, <u>the</u> <u>great</u> <u>explorer</u>, <u>says</u> <u>it</u> <u>could</u> <u>be</u> circumnavigated <u>in</u> forty days.

5. When <u>I</u> <u>turned</u> the <u>key</u> to open my <u>lab</u> <u>door</u>, I <u>thought</u> it <u>would</u> be my usual <u>dull</u> <u>day</u>, until I <u>noticed</u> <u>that</u> <u>my</u> little cucaracha <u>had</u> <u>flopped</u> over on his back, frantically <u>waving</u> his little legs, and <u>I</u> <u>realized</u> that someone had bugged my bug.

6. It <u>was</u> a dark and stormy night, its <u>green</u> <u>clarity</u> <u>diluted</u> by my roommate who, as usual, <u>was</u> <u>making</u> <u>cutting</u> <u>remarks</u> as <u>she</u> <u>drank</u> my <u>scotch</u>.

7. "I <u>hate</u> <u>pineapples</u>," said Tom <u>dolefully</u>.

8. Here's how to make <u>a</u> <u>fortune</u>. Buy fifty <u>female</u> <u>pigs</u> and fifty male deer. Then <u>you</u> <u>will</u> <u>have</u> a hundred sows and <u>bucks</u>.

PHRASES

Phrases are a unit of sentence structure between a word and a sentence. Although a phrase can consist of a single word, a phrase usually consists of two or more words. There are three important components to a phrase.

⇒ **Heads.** A phrase must have a head. The head of a phrase is the obligatory core around which the phrase is built. Four categories usually function as the head of a phrase, thereby allowing for four types of phrases.

1. **NP**   – noun phrase
2. **AP**   – adjective phrase
3. **VP**   – verb phrase
4. **PP**   – prepositional phrase

The head of a noun phrase, of course, is a noun. The head of an adjective phrase, an adjective. The head of a verb phrase, a verb, and the head of a prepositional phrase, a preposition.

⇒ **Specifiers.** A phrase can optionally contain a specifier. Specifiers help to make the meaning of the head more precise. Specifiers mark phrasal boundaries. In English, specifiers occur before the head, thus marking the beginning of a phrase.

1. Determiners   – specify a noun
                               e.g., the, a, these, that ….

2. Adverbs   – specify a verb
                               e.g., always, often, never …

3. Degree words   – specify an adjective or a preposition
                               e.g., very, quite, really …

⇒ **Complements.** A phrase can also optionally contain a complement. Complements provide more information about entities that are implied by the head of the phrase. Like specifiers, complements also provide information on the boundary of a phrase. In English, complements come after the head, thus marking the end of a phrase. Complements are typically other phrases.

REMINDER! REMINDER!

Specifiers can help determine the category to which a word belongs. This is because the type of specifier found in a phrase depends on the category of the head. So, if a word can occur with a determiner, it is a noun, if it occurs with an adverb, it is a verb, and if it occurs with a degree word it is an adjective!

Below are some examples of the different types of phrases.

1. Noun Phrase (NP)

    a. **mud**   – contains only the head noun (**mud**)

    b. **the mud**   – contains a specifier (**the**) and the head noun (**mud**)

    c. **mud**   – contains the head noun (**mud**) and a complement
        on the floor   prepositional phrase (**on the floor**)

    d. **the mud**   – contains a specifier (**the**), the head noun
        on the floor   (**mud**), and a complement prepositional phrase (**on the floor**)

The prepositional phrase **on the floor** consists of a head preposition (**on**) and a complement noun phrase (**the floor**). The noun phrase **the floor** then consists of a specifier (**the**) and a head noun (**floor**).

2. Adjective Phrase (AP)

    a. **happy**   – contains only the head adjective (**happy**)

    b. **very happy**   – contains a specifier (**very**) and the head adjective (**happy**)

    c. **happy with**   – contains the head adjective (**happy**) and a complement
        the results   prepositional phrase (**with the results**)

    d. **very happy**   – contains a specifier (**very**), the head adjective (**happy**),
        with the results   and a complement prepositional phrase (**with the results**)

The prepositional phrase **with the results** consists of a head preposition (**with**) and a complement noun phrase (**the results**). The noun phrase **the results** then consists of a specifier (**the**) and a head noun (**results**).

Notice … Phrases have hierarchical structure!

3. Verb Phrase (VP)

    a. **sings**   – contains only the head verb (**sing**)

    b. **often sings**   – contains a specifier (**often**) and the head verb (**sings**)

    c. **sings a song**   – contains the head verb (**sing**) and a complement noun
                                 phrase (**a song**)

    d. **often sings**   – contains a specifier (**often**), the head verb (**sings**), and a
         a song   a complement noun phrase (**a song**)

The complement noun phrase **a song** consists of a specifier (**a**) and a head noun (**song**).

4. Prepositional Phrase (PP)

    a. **in the car**   – contains the head preposition (**in**) and a complement
                                   noun phrase (**the car**)

    b. **almost in**   – contains a specifier (**almost**), the head preposition (**in**)
         the car   and a complement noun phrase (**the car**)

The complement noun phrase **the car** contains a specifier (**the**) and a head noun (**car**).

Now ... Think of an example of

$\Rightarrow$ A noun phrase containing a specifier, a head noun, and a complement.
$\Rightarrow$ An adjective phrase containing a specifier and a head adjective.
$\Rightarrow$ A verb phrase containing a head verb and a complement.
$\Rightarrow$ A prepositional phrase containing a head preposition and a complement.

REMINDER! REMINDER!

Prepositional phrases are different from the other three types of phrase in that prepositional phrases must always contain a complement, and this complement is usually a noun phrase.

Practice ...

For each of the following phrases, determine the head of the phrase, the specifier, and the complement. Remember that every phrase must have a head but that specifiers and complements are optional! The first is done for you.

	HEAD	SPECIFIER	COMPLEMENT
the rate	rate	the	none
men			
in the barn			
really mean			
worked			
worked at the station			
extremely boring			
that house on the corner			
never walks to the park			
very small			
in the room			
awfully cute			
seldom smiles			
swept the floor			
the poem about love			
pancakes			

Now ... Go back and determine the type of each phrase. Remember: the lexical category of the head determines the type of phrase.

PHRASE STRUCTURE TESTS

There are a number of tests that can be done to determine whether a group of words is or is not a phrase. Three frequently used tests are the Substitution Test, the Movement Test, and the Coordination Test. Be careful though: not every test works for every phrase.

Substitution Test

The Substitution Test states that a group of words is a phrase if it can be substituted with a single word such as 'they', 'do so', or 'there', and still be grammatical. The word used as a substitute also tells you the type of phrase you have.

NP: A noun phrase can be substituted with a pronoun
    e.g.,   **The boys** played in the mud. **They** played in the mud.
        (they = the boys)

VP: A verb phrase can be substituted with 'do so'
    e.g.,   The girls will **play in the mud**, if the boys **do so**.
        (do so = play in the mud)

PP: A prepositional phrase can be substituted with 'there'
    e.g.,   The boys played **in the mud**. The boys played **there**.
        (there = in the mud)

Movement Test

The Movement Test states that a group of words is a phrase if it can be moved to another position in the sentence and still be grammatical.

e.g.,   The children bought candy **at the store.** ⟶
        At the store, the children bought candy.

Coordination Test

According to this test, a group of words is a phrase if it can be joined to another group of words using a conjunction ('and', 'but', 'or') and still be grammatical.

e.g.,   The children **bought candy** and **left the store.**
        – two verb phrases joined with the conjunction 'and'

Try this ... Apply the substitution test to determine which of the bracketed sequences in the following sentences are phrases,

1. [Juanita and Juan] arrived [in San Juan] [on Epiphany].
2. The cabbage [rolls were] salty.
3. They moved [the desk with the wooden top].
4. Little Andrew swallowed [all the pills].
5. The polar bears [were swimming across] the lake.
6. Brendan is [writing a ballad about Canadian soldiers in Cyprus].

Apply the movement test to determine which of the bracketed sequences in the following sentences are phrases.

1. The [army was surrounded] by the enemy.
2. Leona likes [Viennese waltzes and Argentinean tangos].
3. Jean ate his lunch [in the revolving restaurant].
4. Eat, drink, and [be merry for] today will become yesterday.

Use a conjunction (and, but, or) and join each of the following phrases with a phrase of the same type. You might want to first use the substituion test to determine the type of phrase!

1. the new desk
2. assembled the new desk
3. new
4. in a hole
5. rather huge
6. worked on a movie
7. beside the fence
8. really lovely
9. talked to the girls
10. a dentist

Get ready for tree diagrams ...

PHRASE STRUCTURE TREES

Phrases are built using the Merge operation. Merge combines words using the X' (X-bar) schema in which X stands for any head.

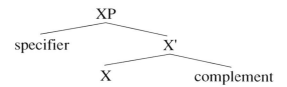

Specifiers attach to the phrasal, XP level, while complements attach to the intermediate X' level. Even though specifiers and complements are optional, X' is always present in the representation of a phrase, called a tree diagram.

Below is an example of a fully diagrammed tree for the noun phrase "a book on Shakespeare" which contains a head, a specifier, and a complement.

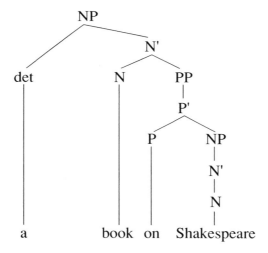

Merge created the above complex phrase by combining the noun phrase "Shakespeare" with the preposition "on" to create the prepositional phrase "on Shakespeare". This phrase was then combined with the noun "book" and the specifier "a" to create the noun phrase "a book on Shakespeare".

Now you try ... Draw tree diagrams for each of the following phrases. Remember: specifiers come before the head, and complements after the head.

1. the rat
2. men
3. in the barn
4. really mean
5. ran
6. ran into the shed
7. rather boring

8. hate those pancakes
9. the house on the corner
10. very small
11. in the room
12. awfully cute
13. seldom smiles
14. swept the floor

15. fond of candy
16. silly
17. the poem about love
18. read the poem
19. jumped over the barn
20. usually eats lunch

QUICK REMINDER:

Use the Substitution Test to help you determine the type of phrase you are dealing with. Remember: the Substitution Test not only tells you if a group of words is or is not a phrase; it can also tell you the type of phrase you have. So … don't just guess!

SENTENCES

A sentence is the largest unit of syntactic analysis. Like a phrase, a sentence consists of a specifier, a head, and a complement.

⇒ **NP.** This noun phrase is typically referred to as the subject and can consist of any of the possibilities we saw during our discussion of phrases. The subject is the specifier of I.

⇒ **I. (Infl).** This is the obligatory head of the sentence, and is used to refer to inflection. There are two possibilities for I: +pst and –pst. +pst is used for sentences in the past tense, and –pst is used for sentences in either the present or future tense.

⇒ **VP.** This verb phrase is typically referred to as the predicate. Like the subject NP, the VP can consist of any of the possibilities we saw during our discussion of phrases. The VP is the complement of I.

Sentences, like phrases, are built according to the X' schema. Since I is the head of a sentence, IP is used to represent this syntactic unit.

Below is an example of a fully diagrammed tree for the sentence "The children read a book".

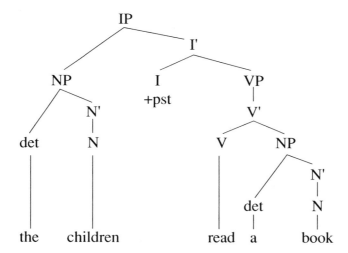

Auxiliary Verbs

A sentence may include an auxiliary verb. Auxiliary verbs can be either modal or non-modal. Modal auxiliary verbs include *will, would, could, should, can, might,* and *may*. Modal auxiliary verbs occupy the I position in a sentence and are –pst. Non-Modal auxiliary verbs include *have* and *be*. Non-modal auxiliaries are a special type of verb that takes a VP as its complement.

Below is an example of a fully diagrammed tree for the sentence, "the children will read a book", which contains a modal auxiliary.

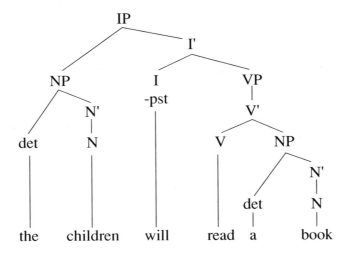

Below is an example of a fully diagrammed tree for the sentence, "the children are reading a book", which contains a non-modal auxiliary.

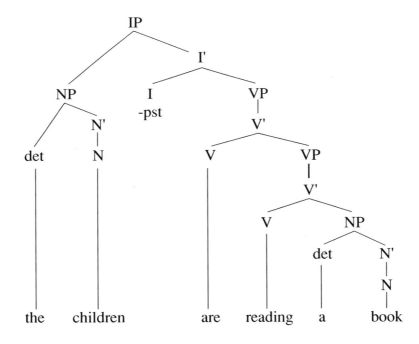

Think! A sentence may contain both a modal and a non-modal auxiliary verb. Consider the sentence "the children will be reading a book". How would the tree for this sentence be different from the tree shown above? Try putting together a tree diagram for this sentence.

The following exercise will give you some practice diagramming sentences. Draw a tree diagram for each of the following sentences.

1. Students often write exams.
2. A penguin walked into the room.
3. Dogs should always go for a walk.
4. Those monsters were hiding under the bed.
5. Abner concealed the document.
6. Marge usually watches the sunset.
7. The children are playing with a dinosaur.
8. That garbage smells.
9. Grandparents may live in condominiums.
10. Carl might have sold that car.

QUICK REMINDER

A noun phrase (NP), a prepositional phrase (PP), or an adjective phrase (AP) are all potential complements of a verb. The particular complement that occurs depends on the verb. Some verbs can take more than one complement! A prepositional phrase (PP) can also function as the complement of a noun.

Complement Clauses

Sentences may themselves function as complements. That is, a sentence can occur in the complement position of a phrase. A sentence contained within a phrase is called a complement clause (CP).

Like other syntactic units, a CP consists of a head, a specifier, and a complement. The head of a CP is a complementizer (C). Complementizers include words such as *that*, *if*, and *whether*. The complement of a complementizer is an IP, a sentence. The specifier position within a CP functions as a landing site for phrases undergoing the Move operation.

Below is a tree diagram for a sentence containing a complement clause within the verb phrase.

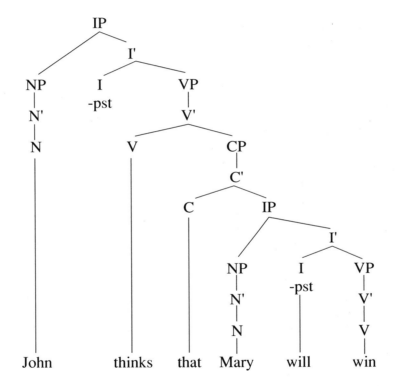

SOME HINTS FOR DRAWING PHRASE STRUCTURE TREES

1. Every sentence (IP) consists of an NP, I, and a VP.

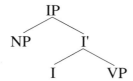

2. Identify the verb. Check if this verb has a specifier and/or a complement. Remember that the optional specifier, an adverb, marks the beginning of the phrase and either the verb or the complement marks the end of the verb phrase.

3. Identify I. I can be either –pst or +pst. +pst is only used if a sentence is in the past tense. Modal auxiliary verbs occur under I, but non-modal auxiliaries occur under the V. Remember these take a VP as their complement.

4. Identify the subject NP. Remember that an optional determiner, the specifier, marks the beginning of this noun phrase, and either the noun or a complement marks the end of the noun phrase.

5. The complement of the verb can be a complement clause (CP).

    Since a CP contains an IP, you will also need to identify and diagram the NP, I, and VP for this embedded IP.

Practice! Practice! Draw a tree diagram for each of the following sentences.

1. Stan hopes that Sean will become a pilot.
2. Nancy believes that aliens exist.
3. Sailors know that they could drown at sea.
4. The realtor wondered whether Louise would sell the house.
5. The passengers thought that the plane would never land.

MORE SENTENCES

The following exercise contains many examples of simple sentences as well as sentences with complement clauses. Draw a tree diagram for each. Watch out: they get harder!

1.   The repairman fixed the watch.

2.   Neighbors can be unfriendly.

3.   Nurses never complain.

4.   The train has left.

5.   The castle fell into the sea.

6.   Those men on the shore saw a signal.

7.   The rabbit hid under the bridge.

8.   The secretary should have mailed the proposal.

9.   Children are very curious.

10.   Flowers bloom in the summer.

11.   That soup tastes really great.

12.   The rabbit will be eating the lilies.

13.   Sally lives in a house by the sea.

14.   The driver of that car is speeding down the highway.

15.   The media has reported that the candidate won the election.

16.   The salesman wondered if those customers would buy the car.

17.   George hoped that Fred would win the car.

18.   Kayleigh usually thinks that playing in the park is fun.

19.   The smugglers perhaps suspected that the police were following them.

20.   The tourists hoped that they might see a whale.

COMPLEMENT OPTIONS

To ensure that the Merge operation builds grammatical sentences, the individual words in a sentence must occur with complements of the right type. For example, many verbs (e.g., throw) require a complement noun phrase and must therefore appear in a structure containing a noun phrase in the complement position. If such a verb were entered into a structure without a noun phrase complement, the result would be an ungrammatical sentence. The complement(s) with which a word can occur are called its complement options. Merge, therefore, combines words into sentences in a manner consistent with both the X' schema and the complement options of the individual words.

Information on the complement options of words along with the meaning and pronunciation of words are found in a speaker's mental lexicon. Information about a word's complement options is often referred to as subcategorization.

Try This! Determine the complement options that the verbs listed below require. Do this by thinking of grammatical and ungrammatical sentences containing the verb.

- panic
- watch
- imagine

- write
- wonder
- play

Nouns, adjectives and prepositions also have restrictions on the types of complements with which they can and cannot occur. Determine the complement options which the following lexical items require.

- pleasure
- with
- contribution

- intelligent
- at
- upset

QUESTIONS

Merge is responsible for building the structure of a sentence and operates in conjunction with both subcategorization information and the X' schema. However, Merge cannot create all the structures of a language. Some structures require a second operation. Move transforms an existing structure (e.g., a statement) into another type of structure (e.g., a question). Move does this by transporting elements from one position in a sentence to another.

There are three important consequences of Move.

⇒ **CP.** Move transports elements to positions with a CP. Auxiliary verbs move to C, while wh-phrases move to the specifier position of C. Every sentence must, therefore, include a CP. If a sentence contains an embedded CP, a complementizer can occur under the C. For all other CPs, information on whether the sentence is a question or a statement is found under the C: if C contains +Q, the structure is a question, and if C is empty, it is a statement.

⇒ **Trace.** Moved elements leave behind a trace (t). A trace records (1) that a movement occurred and (2) where in the structure the moved element originated.

⇒ **Levels of Representation.** Two levels of representation result: deep and surface structure. Merge generates the deep structure. The surface structure is the result of applying any additional operations, such as Move. The surface structure is often called the final syntactic form. If no elements have moved, then the deep and surface structures are the same.

Move operates to create both yes/no and wh-questions.

<u>Yes/No Questions</u>

Yes/No questions are so named because the response to such a question is usually yes or no. Yes/No questions are formed by moving an auxiliary verb, either modal or non-modal, from its position in I to the complementizer position within a CP. This is often called Inversion.

Inversion: Move I to C
                e.g.,   Mary **will** leave → **Will** Mary **t** leave

After Merge:

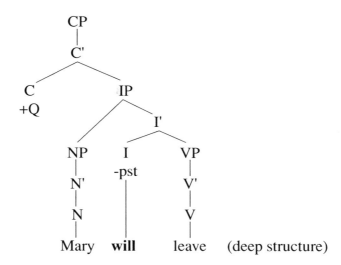

Mary   **will**   leave   (deep structure)

After Inversion:

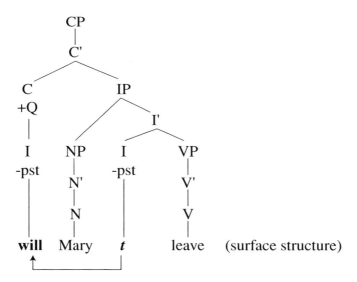

will   Mary   *t*   leave   (surface structure)

Wh-Questions

Wh-questions are so named because they begin with a wh-word (e.g., what, who). Wh-questions are the result of two applications of the move operation: wh-movement and inversion.

Wh-Movement: Move a wh-phrase to the specifier position under CP.

Wh-Movement is followed by Inversion.

e.g.,   George **should** buy *what* → *What* **should** George **t** buy *t*

After Merge:

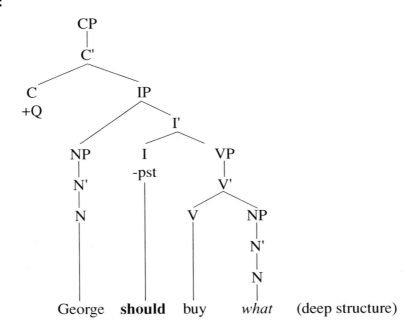

(deep structure)

After Wh-Movement and Inversion:

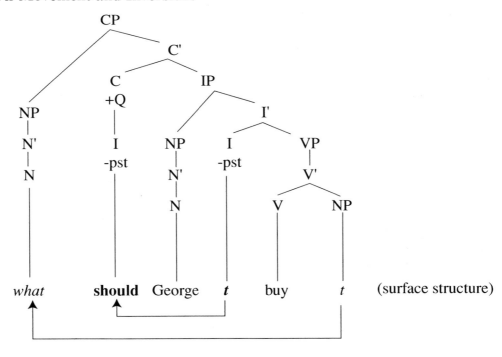

(surface structure)

Try This! For each of the following sentences, draw a tree diagram for both the deep and surface structures. On the surface structure, indicate with arrows the elements that have moved and where they have moved.

1. Can a dog bark?
2. Who can see the shore?
3. Will the trip be fun?
4. Which coat should Joan wear?

| **Remember…** | 1. To include a trace for each movement. |
| | 2. That wh-movement moves an entire phrase. |

OTHER OPERATIONS

Move can also transport a verb to a new position in the sentence. This is often called Verb Raising. As well, new elements can be added to a structure. One example of this operation is Do Insertion.

Verb Raising

Remember there are two types of auxiliaries: modal and non-modal. Modal auxiliaries occur in I and non-modal auxiliaries occur in V. Both types of auxiliaries can be inverted to create a question. However, non-modal auxiliaries must first be moved from V to I, since Inversion moves I to C. This is called Verb Raising.

Verb Raising: Move V to I

e.g.,   Mary **is** leaving → Mary **is t** leaving

After Merge:

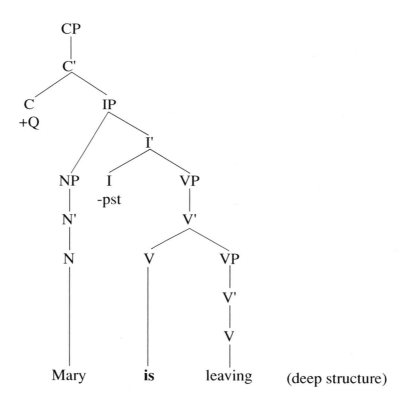

(deep structure)

After Verb Raising:

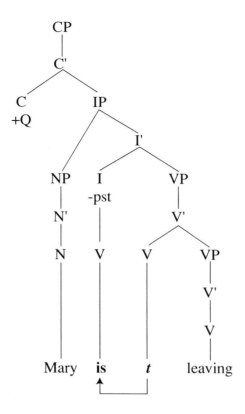

After Inversion:

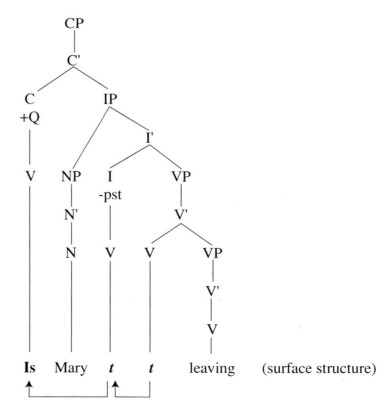

Think!   Verb raising can also occur during the formation of wh-questions.

eg.,   Sylvia **was** thinking *what*. → *What* Sylvia **was** thinking *t* →

What Sylvia **was t** thinking *t* → *What* **was** Sylvia **t t** thinking *t*

Be careful!   Moving the verb to I does not change the word order of the sentence. So, both before and after the verb is moved, the sentence is "what Sylvia was thinking".

Try drawing a tree diagram of both the deep structure and surface structure for the above sentence. You do not need to draw trees for any intermediate structures. Indicate with arrows all of the movements. Do this on the surface structure.

Do Insertion

Auxiliary verbs, whether modal or non-modal, are optional in English. So, many English sentences will not contain auxiliary verbs. Yet, these sentences can still be changed into questions. This is done by inserting "do", "did", or "does" into the sentence.

Do-Insertion: Insert "do" into an empty I position.

eg.,   Mary left → Mary **did** leave → **Did** Mary **t** leave

After Merge:

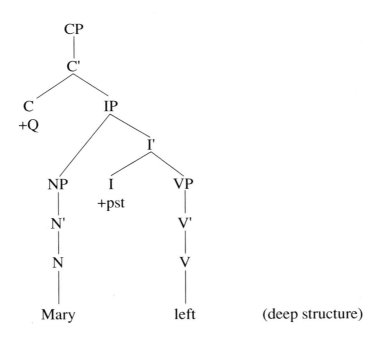

(deep structure)

After Do-Insertion:

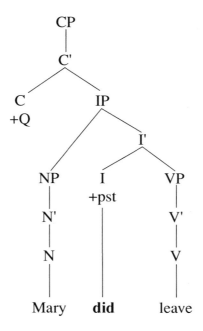

After Inversion:

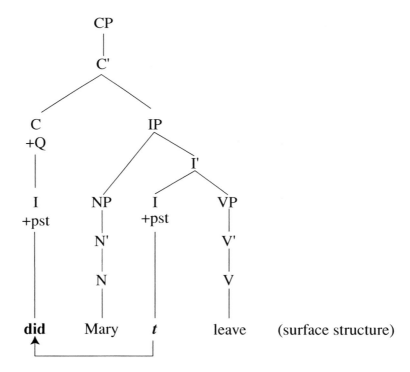

(surface structure)

Think! Do-Insertion can also occur during the formation of wh-questions.

> e.g.,   George bought *what*. $\rightarrow$ *What* George bought *t* $\rightarrow$
>
> *What* George **did** buy *t* $\rightarrow$ *What* **did** George **t** buy *t*

Try drawing a tree diagram of both the deep structure and surface structure for the above sentence. Again, you do not need to draw any intermediate structures. Indicate with arrows all of the movements. Do this on the surface structure.

Try This! For each of the following sentences, draw a tree diagram of both the deep and surface structures.

1. Does Gillian like fish?
2. Who did Jessica invite?
3. Were the elves sweeping the floor?
4. What was Sally painting?

REMINDER! REMINDER!

In English, only the auxiliary verbs (non-modal) can be moved from their position under V to under the I position. This is not true of all languages. For example, in French, any type of verb can be moved into this position.

Some Hints...

You need to be able to determine the deep structure for any sentence you are given, and to do so you need to be able to identify any of the movements that have occurred. Remember, inversion, wh-movement, and verb-raising are all applications of the Move operation. Do-Insertion is also a syntactic operation. You may also have to construct a tree diagram of the deep and surface structures.

Here are some clues to help you identify which movements have occurred, and to put surface structure sentences back into deep structure:

YOU SEE:	YOU THINK:	YOU DO:
A modal auxiliary verb ahead of the subject.	Inversion has taken place.	Put the modal auxiliary back into its deep structure position (I).
A non-modal auxiliary verb ahead of the subject.	Inversion has taken place. Verb Raising has taken place.	Put the non-modal auxiliary back into its deep structure position (V).
A wh-word or phrase.	Wh-Movement has taken place.	Examine each verb in the sentence. Determine if a verb is missing either a subject or an object. Put the wh-word or phrase into that position. Examine each preposition in the sentence. Determine if a preposition is missing its object. Put the wh-word or phrase into that position.
"Do", "Did", or "Does" at the beginning of a sentence, or after a wh-word or phrase.	Do Insertion has taken place.	Remove "do", "did", or "does" from the sentence.

TRANSFORMATION WORKSHEET

Draw a tree diagram of both the deep and surface structure for each of the following sentences. List all movements that have occurred to derive the surface structure.

1.   Can the clown amuse that boy?
2.   Who does the jury blame?
3.   Margo dreamt that Frances might fly to England.
4.   Did Bill sell that house?
5.   Must the musicians play music?
6.   Is that player leaving the team?
7.   What was Joanne eating?
8.   Could the vandals have destroyed those billboards?
9.   Colin thinks that girls never phone George.
10. Who will those immigrants live with?
11. Does Henry think that Harry will survive in the jungle?
12. Who should be preparing the meal?
13. In which box are the dishes?
14. The jury believed that the prisoner was guilty.
15. Would the winner claim the prize?
16. Dianne knew that Tom might like the meal.
17. What does Mary want?
18. Do children like cake?

TWO IMPORTANT REMINDERS:

1.   You are trying to determine which elements have already been moved; therefore, you must **never** move any additional words or phrases!
2.   No movements may have occurred, only one movement may have occurred, or more than one movement may have occurred. To find the deep structure, you need to (1) find all instances of Move, and (2) determine if do-insertion has occurred.

OTHER STRUCTURES

Some other syntactic structures include coordinate structures, relative clauses, and passives. Each of these structures builds on the basic syntactic system (i.e., Merge and Move) for forming sentences.

Coordination

Coordination joins structures together using a conjunction such as *and*, *but*, or *or*. Any level of structure (X, X', or XP) can be joined. Only structures of the same type can be joined together. That is, a NP must be conjoined with another NP. If structures of different types are joined, the result is an ungrammatical structure. Finally, conjoining structures results in a larger structure of the same type. So, joining two NPs together results in a larger NP.

e.g.,   Vs: $[draw]_V$ and $[color]_V$ those pictures
        N's: that $[car]_{N'}$ and $[truck]_{N'}$
        PPs: $[up the stairs]_{PP}$ and $[into the hallway]_{PP}$

Relative Clauses

A relative clause is a type of complement clause (CP) that provides information about a preceding noun. Relative clauses can modify either subjects or objects. Relative clauses are similar to wh-questions: both begin with a wh-word and both involve wh-movement. And like in wh-questions, wh-movement can move a wh-word or phrase from either the subject or the direct object position.

e.g.,   The girl $[who lives across the street]_{CP}$ came for a visit.
                - modifies the noun "girl"

        Norm brought the flowers $[which Sue has]_{CP}$.
                - modifiers the noun "flowers"

Passives

A sentence may be either active or passive. In an active sentence, the agent or doer of the action occurs in the subject position. In a passive sentence, this agent may either be absent or present within the VP as the object of a preposition. In a passive sentence, the direct object usually functions as the subject of the sentence.   Passive sentences are formed using NP Movement, another type of Move. NP Movement transports an object from its deep structure position as a complement of the verb to an empty subject position.

e.g.,   **Active:**   The chef prepared the meal.

        Passive: The meal was prepared. / The meal was prepared by the chef.

Exercise! The following exercises will give you some practice with identifying co-ordinate structures, relative clauses, and passives.

1. For each of the following coordinate structures, determine the category of the structures that have been joined together.

   a. Stephen watched television but Gloria listened to the radio.
   b. Terry drove the Ninja-Turtle and the Monster-Mutt.
   c. Bill believes that the world is round and that the sun is hot.
   d. Andrea usually eats dinner and goes to bed.

2. Each of the following sentences contains a relative clause. Put brackets around this clause. Remember: a relative clause is a CP.

   a. The movie which Henry likes is really awful.
   b. Sarah was talking to the cyclist who won the race.
   c. The building which Winston designed may be demolished.

3. Decide if each of the following sentences is active or passive. Remember: a passive sentence does not necessarily include an agent.

   a. That lamp could be fixed.
   b. Those tigers were trained by a professional.
   c. The company should make a donation.
   d. The winner was given a prize.

REVIEW REVIEW!! If you can do the following, then you've conquered syntax:

- describe the differences between lexical and non-lexical categories
- assign words to their syntactic category
- determine if a group of words is or is not a phrase
- identify and diagram phrases
- diagram sentences, including those with complement clauses
- determine complement options
- understand the Merge and Move operations
- spot yes/no and wh-questions
- spot inversion, wh-movement, verb-raising, and do-insertion
- find the deep structure of a sentence
- recognize coordinate structures, relative clauses, and passives

QUESTIONS? PROBLEMS? DIFFICULTIES?

_____

_____

_____

_____

_____

_____

_____

_____

_____

_____

_____

CHAPTER 6. SEMANTICS:
THE ANALYSIS OF MEANING

Semantics is the study of meaning in human language. Meaning refers, very generally, to the content of an utterance.

Important concepts and topics in this chapter include:

1. semantic relations
2. meaning
3. concepts
4. lexicalization
5. grammaticization
6. ambiguity
7. thematic roles
8. pragmatics
9. conversation

SEMANTIC RELATIONS

Determining the semantic relations that exist between words, phrases, and sentences constitutes one of the basic analytic tools available for evaluating meaning.

<u>Relations between words:</u>

RELATION	DEFINITION
Synonymy	Words which have similar meanings. e.g., vacation / holiday
Antonymy	Words which have opposite meanings. e.g., hot / cold
Polysemy	A word that has two or more related meanings. e.g., bright (shining, or intelligent)
Homophony	Two words with the same form (i.e. pronunciation) but two distinct different meanings e.g., pen (a writing instrument or a small cage)

Relations between sentences:

RELATION	DEFINITION
Paraphrase	Two sentences that have different forms, but very similar meanings. e.g., The cat ate the mouse. The mouse was eaten by the cat.
Entailment	Two sentences in which the truth of the first implies the truth of the second, but the truth of the second does not necessarily imply the truth of the first. e.g., George killed the burglar. The burglar is dead.
Contradiction	Two sentences such that if one is true, then the second must be false. e.g., George is rich. George lives in a shelter

Try this! For each of the following, identify the relation that exists between either the words or the sentences. The first is done for you!

1. test
   exam   synonyms _____

2. Mary sang a solo.
   A solo was sung by Mary.   _____

3. bug (insect)
   bug (microphone)   _____

4. Sam is a widower.
   Sam's wife is alive.   _____

5. The bear attacked a camper.
   The camper is injured.   _____

6. parent
   offspring   _____

7. George gave Sally the book.
    George gave the book to Sally.   _____

8. Nancy brought salmon for dinner.
    There is nothing to eat for dinner.   _____

9. hungry
    famished   _____

10. steak (a piece of meat)
    stake (a sharp piece of wood)   _____

REMINDER! REMINDER!

Polysems and homophones are not the same. Polysems have related meanings while homophones have unrelated meanings. Homophones need not have identical spelling!

MEANING

As native speakers of a language, we all know the meaning of a great many words in our language. And if we come across a word whose meaning is unknown to us, we can always look it up in a dictionary! But, to understand the dictionary definition, we need to understand the meanings of the words making up the definition. It is easier to determine the semantic relations between words than the precise meaning of a word! Examples of some theories of meaning are given below.

Connotation

This theory states that the meaning of a word is simply the set of associations that the use of the word evokes. Think about what connotations the words *spring*, *bridge* and *Hawaii* evoke.

Denotation

This theory states that the meaning of a word is not the set of associations it evokes, but rather the entity to which it refers; that is, its denotation or referent. Think about what denotation the words *spring*, *bridge* and *Hawaii* have.

Extension and Intension

This theory attempts to combine the first two. Extension refers to the referent of a word, and intension to the associations it evokes. Thus, the meaning of a word includes both its extension and its intension.

Componential Analysis

This theory is based on the idea that meaning can be decomposed into smaller semantic units. These units of meaning are called features. Semantic features can be combined to group entities into classes. For example, the semantic features [+living, +human, –adult] gives us the category of children. Think about how you might decompose the meaning of the words *spring*, *bridge*, and *Hawaii* into semantic features.

Componential analysis allows us to make generalizations. For example, features of a verb's meaning can be relevant when it comes to choosing the phrases to go along with that verb to form a verb phrase.

Think ... What difficulties do connotation, denotation, extension, intension, and componential analysis have in determining what meaning is?

Practice! Practice! For each of the following words, attempt to define their meaning according to the theories of connotation, denotation, and extension and intension presented above.

1. summer
2. a linguistics instructor
3. grass

Identify the types of phrases with which the verbs in A and B can occur.   What difference in meaning between the verbs in A and the verbs in B determines the type of complement the verbs require?

A	B
sweep	crawl
kick	fell

Examine the following two groups of words and determine the semantic feature(s) each group has in common. What semantic feature(s) are different between members of each group? What about between the two groups?

Group A: grandmother / mother / daughter /   widow
Group B: grandfather /   father /   son   / widower

Now ... try doing a componential analysis for: ⇒ ewe and lamb
                                                          ⇒ mare, filly, and colt

What difficulties did you have in decomposing the meanings of the nouns?

CONCEPTS

Linguists use the term 'concepts' to refer to the system we use to identify, classify, and organize all elements of our many and varied experiences. Our conceptual system reveals how meaning is expressed through language.

Fuzzy Concepts

Fuzzy concepts are concepts which can differ from person to person. They have no clearcut boundaries. Think about how much something has to cost before you would consider it expensive.

Graded Membership

Concepts have internal structure. Members of a concept can be graded according to how typical they are within that concept. The most typical member is selected as the prototype. Other members are arranged around the prototype. Members having more properties in common with the prototype occur closer to the prototype. Members sharing fewer properties occur further away from the prototype.

Metaphor

The concepts expressed by language do not exist in isolation, but are interconnected and associated. Metaphors, the understanding of one concept in terms of another, can be used to make these connections. For example, emotions are often compared to spatial terms such as 'up' or 'down' (e.g., George is feeling down today). Think of a metaphor that attributes animal-like properties to people.

Lexicalization

Lexicalization refers to the process whereby concepts are encoded into the words of a language. How concepts combine for lexicalization varies from language to language. For example, in English, many verbs such as 'roll', 'slide', and 'limp' contain both the idea of motion and the manner in which the motion occurs. Other languages (e.g., Spanish) cannot use one word to express both concepts, but require separate words for each. Spanish verbs of motion, though, express both the concept of motion and the direction of its path!

Grammaticization

Grammaticization refers to concepts which are expressed as affixes or non-lexical categories. Concepts such as tense, number, and negation are often grammaticized across languages. However, many other concepts can also be grammaticized. For example, statements in Hidats are accompanied by a morpheme that indicates the evidence for its truth (i.e. certainty, common knowledge, or unknown). Think about the different ways in which negation has been grammaticized in English.

Exercise! Exercise! For each of the following concepts, determine whether they are fuzzy, graded, or have been grammaticized.

1. the comparative and superlative
2. cats
3. mountains
4. time
5. vegetables

For any of the above that exhibit a graded membership, determine the member which is prototypical for you. How might this differ from person to person?

Quite often, languages contain different forms of grammaticized affixes or functional categories. Consider the data below from Cree involving possession and answer the questions that follow.

	Noun	**My Noun**	**Gloss**
1.	mispiton	nispiton	arm
2.	tʃima:n	nitʃima:n	canoe
3.	miski:sik	niski:sik	eye
4.	mo:htawiya	no:htawiya	father
5.	mo:ka:wiya	no:ka:wiya	mother
6.	astotin	nitastotin	cap

What are the two different (morphological) ways of indicating possession? What is the semantic basis for this difference? Try to relate it to different kinds of possession: which of the above could you give away and which couldn't you?

Some more to try!

1. The language data below illustrates differences in the use of singular and plural prefixes in Swahili. Group the nouns into classes based on their use of the different prefixes. What is the semantic basis for your grouping?

	sg.	pl.	Gloss
1.	mtoto	watoto	child
2.	mhindi	mihindi	corn
3.	kikombe	vikombe	hair
4.	mkindu	mikindu	date palm
5.	mfigili	mifigili	radish
6.	mwalimu	wawalimu	teacher
7.	kioo	vioo	mirror
8.	mume	waume	husband
9.	kikapu	vikapu	basket
10.	mboga	miboga	pumpkin

2. **German.** German neuter nouns can occur in a prepositional phrase in either the dative case (definite article dem) or in the accusative case (definite article das). Examine the following sentences and determine the semantic basis for the choice of either the dative or accusative case.

    1. Monika arbeitet in dem Kaffeehaus. (Monika works in the coffeehouse.)
        Stefan kommt in das Kaffeehause. (Stefan comes into the coffeehouse.)

    2. Ritas Stuhl steht neben dem Fenster. (Rita's stool stands next to the window.)
        Jan stellt seinen Stuhl neben das Fenster. (Jan puts his chair next to the window.)

    3. Ein Schuh steht unter dem Bett. (A shoe is under the bed.)
        Kurt stellt den anderen Schuh unter das Bett. (Kurt puts the other shoe under the bed.)

    4. Ilsa ist in dem Wohnzimmer. (Ilsa is in the living-room.)
        Armin geht in das Wohnzimmer. (Armin goes into the living-room.)

    What concept is contained in the German articles that is not found in English articles?

AMBIGUITY

A sentence is ambiguous when it has more than one meaning. There are two main types of ambiguity.

⇒ **Lexical ambiguity.** This type of ambiguity results from one word in the sentence having more than one meaning. Polysemy and homophony give us lexical ambiguity. For example, the sentence ***The glasses are on the table.*** has two meanings: (1) the drinking glasses are on the table, and (2) the eye-glasses are on the table. The ambiguity arises because the word 'glasses' has two possible meanings.

⇒ **Structural ambiguity.** This type of ambiguity results from a phrase in the sentence having more than one possible structure. Each possible structure is associated with a different interpretation, or reading.

Consider the ambiguous sentence ***The surface was painted with red flowers and leaves.*** In this sentence, the ambiguity is found within the noun phrase, which will, therefore, have two different syntactic structures.

<u>Reading One:</u>   Both the flowers and the leaves are red.

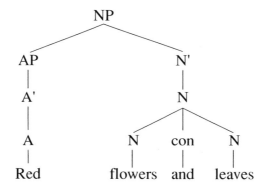

<u>Reading Two:</u>   Only the flowers are red.

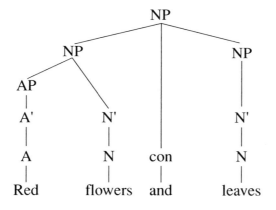

Ambiguity can also be found within the verb phrase. Consider the ambiguous sentence *Sam ate the cake in the kitchen.* In this example, the verb phrase has two different possible structures.

Reading One: Sam ate the cake that was in the kitchen.

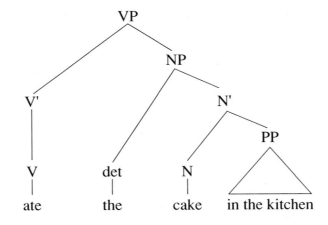

Reading Two: Sam was in the kitchen eating cake.

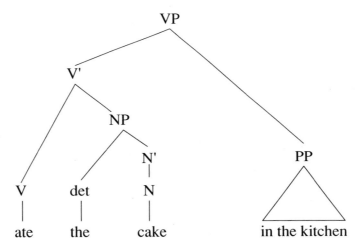

SOME HINTS FOR IDENTIFYING AMBIGUITY!

1. Determine if the ambiguity is coming from one word in the sentence (lexical) or from more than one possible combination of the words in the sentence (structural).
2. For lexical ambiguity, identify the word that is ambiguous and determine the two (or more) possible meanings of the word.
3. For structural ambiguity, determine the phrase containing the ambiguity (usually noun or verb), and the possible meanings. Match each meaning with a different syntactic structure.

Try this! Each of the sentences below is ambiguous. For each sentence, state whether the ambiguity is lexical or structural and provide an unambiguous phrase or sentence for each possible meaning.

1. Cool beer and wine are what we want.
2. I met the woman standing by the water cooler.
3. Parliament passed a dangerous drug bill.
4. Businessmen like black and white ties.
5. George and Harry or Fred will draw the picture.
6. I want to look at the pictures in the attic.
7. The instructor left his key in the office.

Now ... go back over the sentences, and for all those that are structurally ambiguous, draw a tree structure for each possible interpretation, or reading. You might want to start by first identifying which phrase contains the ambiguity. Remember that each interpretation will have a different structure!

THEMATIC ROLES

To interpret sentences, we need to know who is doing the action, what is undergoing the action, the starting point of the action, etc.   Thematic, or theta, roles capture the relation between a sentence and the event it describes.

There are three important properties of thematic roles.

⇒ **Common Thematic Roles.** Some of the common thematic roles include

Agent (actor)	The entity performing an action.
Theme	The entity undergoing an action.
Source	The starting point of a movement.
Goal	The end point of a movement.
Location	The place where an action occurs.

⇒ **Thematic Role Assignment.** Thematic roles are assigned to noun phrases based on their position within the sentence. Typically, verbs and prepositions assign thematic roles.

Verbs...	Assign the agent role (if it has one) to its subject noun phrase Assign the theme role (if it has one) to its complement noun phrase
Prepositions...	Assign a thematic role (the specific one depends on the preposition) to its complement noun phrase

Knowledge of the thematic roles that individual verbs and prepositions assign is stored in our mental lexicon.

Thematic role assignment can be diagrammed as follows:

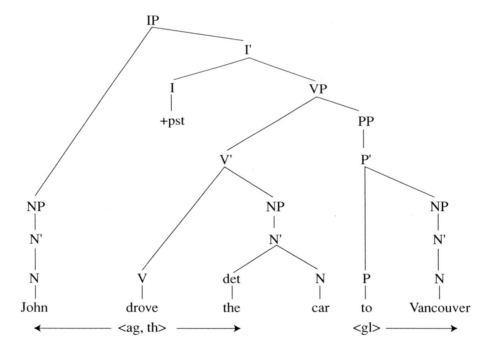

In the above sentence, the verb 'drove' assigns the agent role <ag> to the noun phrase 'John' and the theme role <th> to the noun phrase 'the car', while the preposition 'to' assigns the goal role <gl> to the noun phrase 'Vancouver'.

⇒ **Thematic Roles and Deep Structure.** Thematic roles are assigned at deep structure. A noun phrase's position in the syntactic representation that is the result of the Merge Operation determines its thematic role. For example, the wh-question ***What did George lose?*** has the deep structure ***George lost what.*** Accordingly, the verb 'lost' assigns the agent role to 'George' and the theme role to 'what'. 'What' retains this role even after the Move Operation changes its position in the structure!

Exercise! For each of the following sentences, identify all the noun phrases and the thematic role assigned to each noun phrase.

1. Sarah drove that bus from Toronto to St. John's.
2. The children are eating their ice-cream with spoons.
3. Which shoes did you buy at the store?
4. The cat was chased around the garden by a large dog.
5. The boys walked to the park.
6. Sally mailed her nephew a parcel.
7. What did Bill leave at your house?
8. The letter was sent.
9. Ginger scribbled her address on the paper with a pen.
10. The minister is in the pulpit.

Now ... go back through each sentence and for each thematic role, determine the verb or preposition that assigned the role. Make sure you put any sentences in which Move has applied into the deep structure first. Remember: the deep structure is the result of Merge.

REMINDER! REMINDER!

The interpretation of a sentence involves many factors. Both the syntactic structure and the meaning of the words in that structure contribute to the meaning of a sentence. The construction in which words occur may also contribute to the meaning of the sentence. As well, the role each NP in a sentence plays must be interpreted. And, when words in a sentence can be combined in more than one way, ambiguity results!

PRAGMATICS

Besides the structure of a sentence and the thematic roles assigned to the noun phrases within a sentence, there are many other factors involved in sentence interpretation. Pragmatics is the study of the role other necessary information has in sentence interpretation.

Beliefs and Attitudes

Non-linguistic knowledge can be used to interpret elements within a sentence. For example, in the sentence *City Council denied the demonstrators a permit because they advocated violence*, we assume that the pronoun 'they' refers to the demonstrators and not the council members because of our beliefs about demonstrators. If we change the verb from *advocate* to *abhor*, we now assume that 'they' refers to the council and not the demonstrators. Again, this is based on our world beliefs.

Presupposition

Presupposition refers to the assumption or belief implied by the use of a particular word. For example, in the sentence *John admitted that the soccer team had won the game*, the use of the verb 'admit' presupposes or implies that the team had actually won.

Setting / Deictics

The form and interpretation of some words depends on the location of the speaker and listener within a particular setting. These words are called deictics. Some examples of English deictics include *here / there* and *this / that*. 'here' and 'this' are used to refer to items close to the speaker, while 'there' and 'that' are used to refer to items close to the listener.

Discourse / Topic

Many sentences can only be interpreted in reference to information contained in preceding sentences. Discourse is the term used to describe the connected series of utterances which are produced during a conversation, lecture, story, or other type of speech act. Old (given) information refers to knowledge that is known to the participants of the speech act, while new information refers to knowledge that is introduced into the discourse for the first time. The topic is what a sentence or discourse is all about. Often the subject of a sentence corresponds to the topic. Some languages (e.g., Japanese) use a special affix to indicate the topic of the discourse.

Practice! Practice! Sentences can be difficult to interpret because they are ungrammatical, because they violate our knowledge of the world, or because they contain words which have no known referent. For each of the following sentences, identify why it is hard to interpret.

1. Our ten-month-old son is six feet tall.
2. Mike red bought car a.
3. Palm trees grow vigorously at the North Pole.
4. Radiculus glautons are found in the soil.
5. The bumble-bee picked up the cat and flew back to the hive with it.

⇒ Go back and reconsider #4. What meaning might you assign to the unknown words in this sentence? What about the meaning of the overall sentence?

⇒ Why might the sentence ***His mother wants you to be a doctor*** be difficult to interpret as a stand-alone sentence (i.e., not as part of a discourse)?

CONVERSATION

We use words and sentences to convey messages. And we often do this by having a conversation with someone. Conversations have rules. These rules refer to our understanding of how language is used to convey messages. Our knowledge of these rules also contributes to our interpretation of utterances.

⇒ **General Principle.** The general principle guiding all conversational interactions is the Cooperative Principle.

> ### Cooperative Principle
>
> Make your contribution appropriate to the conversation

⇒ **Specific Maxims.** Conversations also have more specific guidelines. These guidelines are called specific maxims, and if we follow these maxims, then we have adhered to the Cooperative Principle. Of course, these maxims can be violated for specific purposes.

> ### Maxim of Relation
>
> Make your contribution relevant to the conversation.
>
> ### Maxim of Quality
> Make your contribution truthful.
>
> ### Maxim of Quantity
> Make your contribution only as informative as required
>
> ### Maxim of Manner
> Make your contribution unambiguous, clear and logical.

⇒ **Conversational Implicature.** During the course of a conversation, we are often able to make inferences about what is meant, but was not actually said. Consider, for example, the following interaction:

> Mike: How did you do on the last exam?
> Jim: Want to come with me to the Registrar's Office?

In the above example, Jim violates the Maxim of Relation, and even though he doesn't actually say how he did on the exam, it can be inferred from his response that he did rather badly!

Try This!!

You've just missed your bus and are standing at the bus-stop waiting for the next bus. The time is 2 PM and the next bus is due at 2:15 PM, but you don't know that. You ask someone at the bus-stop when the next bus is due and receive several replies. Each reply you receive may or may not violate one or more conversational maxims. For each reply, identify which maxim(s), if any, have been violated.

1. When's the next bus?
   At 2:30. (He's lying.)

   _____

2. When's the next bus?
   When I was little I was obsessed with buses. I wanted to be a bus-driver. I had hundreds of different kinds of buses. Little buses, big buses, red buses, blue buses and even double-deck-ered buses. Did you know that in England, many buses are double-deckered? I have made a study of buses. I think the next bus will be here in 15 minutes. Did you know that in India there are no buses? Did you know I wanted to be a bus driver? Did you know …

   _____

3. When's the next bus?
   Let me think! If the last bus was here at 1:50 and if they run every 20 minutes or so, then the next bus should be here at 2:10. (He has no idea.)

   _____

4. When's the next bus?
   At 2:15, but if we were in Newfoundland that would be 2:45.

   _____

5. When's the next bus?
   I don't know. (He's telling the truth.)

   _____

REVIEW! REVIEW! Make sure you can:

- identify the semantic relations between words (4)
- identify the semantic relations between sentences (3)
- define connotation, denotation, extension and intension
- do componential analysis
- spot fuzzy concepts, grammaticized concepts, and lexicalized concepts
- spot the semantic basis for different word classes
- spot lexical ambiguity
- spot and represent structural ambiguity
- identify noun phrases and their thematic roles
- identify the effect of world knowledge in sentence interpretation
- identify when presupposition occurs in sentence interpretation
- spot the different forms of deictic terms
- identify conversational principles and maxims

QUESTIONS? PROBLEMS? DIFFICULTIES?

_____

_____

_____

_____

_____

_____

_____

_____

_____

_____

_____

CHAPTER 7: HISTORICAL LINGUISTICS: THE STUDY OF LANGUAGE CHANGE

Historical Linguistics studies the principles governing language change. This branch of linguistics is concerned with both the description and explanation of language change. Some of the important topics and concepts in this chapter include:

1. Sound Change
2. Phonological Change
3. Morphological Change
4. Syntactic Change
5. Lexical Change
6. Semantic Change
7. Language Reconstruction
8. Indo-European
9. Development of English
10. Naturalness and Typology

LANGUAGE CHANGE

Some important points concerning language change include:

⇒ Language is always changing. However, for a particular change to take hold, it must be accepted by the language community as a whole.

⇒ Language change is regular and systematic. Some changes affect all words without exception. Other changes begin in a small number of words in the speech of a small number of speakers. These changes may gradually spread through both the vocabulary and the population.

⇒ Languages change because of the way language is acquired. Children are not born with a complete grammar, but must construct a grammar based on the language they are exposed to. Therefore, changes will occur from one generation to the next, and because all children have the same genetic capabilities for language, and construct their grammars in similar fashions, the same patterns of change repeat both within and across languages.

⇒ Causes of language change include articulatory simplification, spelling, reanalysis, analogy, and language contact.

SEQUENTIAL SOUND CHANGE

While all aspects of a language's structure can change, sound change is often the most noticeable. There are many types of sound change that can occur, but most sound changes involve sequences of segments. The major types of sequential sound changes are outlined in the boxes below.

⇒ **Assimilation.** Assimilation involves sounds changing to become more like the nearby sounds. Assimilation increases the efficiency of the articulations involved in producing the sequence of sounds. Such an increase in efficiency can result in articulatory simplification.

Some common examples include:

a. Place of Articulation Assimilation A sound becomes similar to a nearby sound in terms of place of articulation.	a. Old Span [semda] > Mod Span [senda]
b. Manner of Articulation Assimilation A consonant changes its manner of articulation to be like a nearby sound.	b. Early Old Eng [stefn] > Later Old Eng [stemn]
c. Total Assimilation A sound assimilates totally to a following sound.	c. Lat [septem] > Italian [settem]
d. Nasalization A vowel becomes nasal near a nasal sound.	d. Lat [vinu] > Old Fr. [vĩn]
e. Palatalization An alveolar, dental or velar stop's place of articulation becomes more palatal. This usually occurs near a sound that is made with the tongue at or near the hard palate—usually [y], [i], or [j].	e. Old Eng [kirike] > Mid. Eng [ʧirʧe]

Palatalization is often the first step in the creation of an affricate. The type of change in which a palatalized stop becomes an affricate is called **affrication**. Like palatalization, affrication is often induced by front vowels or [j].

The above assimilatory changes most often affect adjacent segments; however, assimilation can apply at a distance. **Umlaut**, which is responsible for irregular plurals such as goose/geese, is an example of such a change.

⇒ **Weakening.** Full vowels have a tendency to reduce, or weaken, to a schwa-like vowel before they delete. Consonants can be defined along a strength hierarchy, shown below.

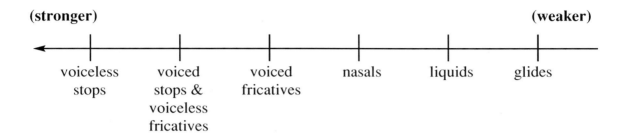

(stronger)   **(weaker)**

voiceless	voiced	voiced	nasals	liquids	glides
stops	stops &	fricatives			
	voiceless				
	fricatives				

Geminate (long) consonants are stronger than their non-geminate counterparts. The tendency over time is for consonants to weaken along a path determined by the above hierarchy.

Some common examples include:

VOWEL WEAKENING
 	
a. Vowel Reduction
     A vowel reduces to schwa.
     This often occurs in unstressed syllables.
	a. Old Eng [na:ma] >
	     Mid Eng [na:mə]

CONSONANTAL WEAKENING
 	
a. Degemination
     A long sound becomes short.
     This is usually the first step in the
     weakening of consonants.
 	
b. Frication
     A stop weakens to a fricative. This
     often occurs between vowels.
 	
c. Voicing
     Voiceless stops or fricatives weaken to
     voiced stops or fricatives.
 	
d. Rhotacism
     A fairly common type of weakening in
     which [z] weakens to [r].
	a. Lat [mittere] >
	     Span [meter]
	
	b. Old Span [maduro] >
	     Span. [maðuro]
	
	c. Lat [maturus] >
	     Old Span [maduro]
	
	d. Gothic 'mai [z] a' >
	     English 'mo [r] e'

Consonants can also strengthen. Glides often strengthen to an affricate. This process is called **Glide Strengthening** and is common in word initial position.

⇒ **Deletion.** Deletion is often the end result of the weakening processes outlined in the previous box. Both vowels and consonants may delete. Vowels are often subject to deletion when they occur in unstressed syllables.

Some common examples include:

VOWEL DELETION
 	
 a. Apocope
  The deletion of a word-final vowel.
 	
 b. Syncope
  The deletion of a word-internal vowel
	a. Mid Eng [na:mə] >
	  Mod Eng [nem]
	
	 b. Lat [vivər] >
	  Fr. [vivr]

CONSONANT DELETION
 	
 a. Consonant Deletion
  Consonants often delete when they occur
  as part of a consonant cluster, or as the
  final consonant in a word, or as the last
  step after several weakening processes.
	a. Old Eng [kne:] >
	  Mod Eng [ni]

⇒ **Others.** There are other types of sound changes as well, many of which will be familiar to you from the Phonology chapter! These types of sound changes are not as frequent as those already presented, but like assimilation also tend to have the overall effect of making sequences of sounds easier to articulate. Also like assimilation, these changes can affect adjacent segments or segments at a distance.

Some common examples include:

a. Dissimilation
  A sound becomes less like a nearby sound.
  This often occurs so that a sequence of
  sounds is easier to articulate or perceive.
	a. Lat [anma] >
	  Span [alma]

b. Epenthesis
  A sound is inserted. This usually occurs
  to break up a consonant cluster that is
  hard to pronounce.
	b. Old Eng [bræməl] >
	  Mod Eng [bræmbəl]

c. Metathesis
  The position of two sounds has changed
  relative to each other.
	c. Lat 'mira [k] u [l] um' >
	  Span 'mi [l] a [g] ro'

OTHER TYPES OF SOUND CHANGE

The changes considered so far have all involved segments changing under the influence of nearby, although not necessarily adjacent, segments. There are two other common types of sound change: segmental and auditory.

⇒ **Segmental Change.**   Segmental change involves a change within the segment itself. Segmental change often involves affricates. Affricates are considered a complex segment, since they consist of a stop and a fricative, and complex segments often simplify over time

One common example is given below:

a.   Deaffrication
    An affricate becomes a fricative by
    eliminating the stop portion of the affricate.
	a. Old French [ts]ent >
	    French [s]ent

⇒ **Auditory Change.** In addition to the articulatory considerations typically involved in sound change, auditory factors can also have an influence.

One common example is given below.

a.   Substitution
    One segment is replaced with
    a similar sounding segment.
	a. Middle Eng lau [x] >
	    English lau [f]

Get ready to identify sound changes …

NAME THAT SOUND CHANGE

Each of the following exemplifies one or more sound changes. The older form is on the left, and the newer, more recent form on the right. Identify the sound change that has taken place for each of the underlined sound(s).

1. Proto-Quechua   [cum<u>p</u>i]   >   Tena   [cum<u>b</u>i]

    _____

2. Old English   [<u>hl</u>af]   >   Modern English   [<u>l</u>of]

    _____

3. Latin   [mar<u>e</u>]   >   Portuguese   [mar]

    _____

4. Proto-Slavic   [<u>k</u>emerai]   >   Russian   [<u>ʧ</u>emer]

    _____

5. Proto-Tupi-Guarani   [puʔ<u>am</u>]   >   Guarani   [puʔ<u>ã</u>]

    _____

6. Latin   [orn<u>a</u>mentum]   >   Old French   [orn<u>ə</u>ment]

    _____

7. Old English   [<u>kn</u>o<u>tt</u>a]   >   Mod. English   [<u>n</u>ɑt]

    _____

8. Proto-Germanic   [doːm<u>az</u>]   >   Old Icelandic   [doːm<u>r</u>]

    _____

9. Latin   [venre]   >   Spanish   [ven<u>d</u>re]

    _____

10. Early Latin   [<u>in</u>possibili<u>ss</u>]   >   Latin   [<u>im</u>possibili<u>s</u>]

    _____

11.   Proto-Bantu   [mu<u>ki</u>ːpa]   >   Swahili   [mʃipa]

---

12.   Proto-Romance   [se<u>k</u>uru]   >   Spanish   [se<u>g</u>uru]

---

13.   Latin   [pe<u>kk</u>a<u>t</u>um]   >   [pe<u>k</u>aθo]   >   [pe<u>k</u>a<u>ð</u>o]

---

14.   Proto-Romance   [biskɔ<u>k</u>tu]   >   Latin   [bisko<u>tt</u>o]

Now... Sound change tends to occur in a step-by-step fashion, so a single sound can often be subject to a number of different sound changes. But, these multiple sound changes are often not visible in the resulting form.

Examine the change below that affected the word 'good' in the development from Proto-Germanic to Old Icelandic and see if you can identify all the changes, including any intermediate but not visible changes that have affected the underlined sounds.

Proto-Germanic   [goː<u>das</u>]   Old Icelandic [goː<u>ð</u>r]

PHONOLOGICAL SOUND CHANGE

The sound changes described in the previous sections can influence a language's phonological inventory. That is, they can add, eliminate, or rearrange the phonemes within a language.

⇒ **Phonological Splits.** A phonological split adds phonemes to a language's phonological inventory. In a phonological split, allophones of the same phoneme come to contrast with each other. This is often caused by a loss of the conditioning environment. That is, sounds that were once predictable are no longer predictable, and are, therefore, phonemic.

Consider the following example in the development of English.

Old English: In Old English, /n/ had two allophones:
    – [ŋ] occurred before velar stops
    – [n] occurred elsewhere

So ... a word like 'sing' was pronounced as [sɪŋg].

Middle English: Consonant Deletion applied to remove [g] at the end of a word (after a nasal consonant). This created a minimal pair between 'sing', now pronounced as [siŋ], and 'sin', pronounced as [sɪn]. And minimal pairs tell us that sounds contrast. [ŋ] and [n] are now separate phonemes.

This split can be diagrammed as follows:

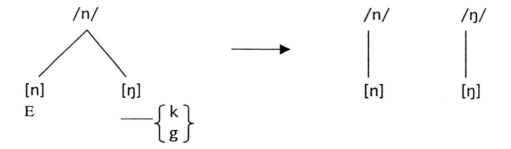

Think ... Spelling often lags behind sound change. We still spell 'sing' with the final 'g' even though it is now silent. Many silent letters in our English spelling system are a reflection of older pronunciations!

⇒ **Phonological Mergers.** While a phonological split adds phonemes to a language, a phonological merger reduces the number of contrasts.

A good example of a phonological merger comes from Cockney English. In Cockney English, the interdental and labiodental fricatives have merged. That is, all instances of [θ] and [ð] have become [f] and [v] respectively. In effect, [θ] and [ð] have been lost from the phonemic inventory.

⇒ **Phonological Shifts.** A phonological shift does not add to or diminish a language's phonemic inventory. Rather, some of the phonemes are reorganized with respect to each other.

The Great English Vowel Shift, beginning in Middle English, is a well-known example of this. The chart below gives the Middle English long vowels before the vowel shift occurred.

	FRONT	CENTRAL	BACK
HIGH	iː		uː
MID	eː ɛː		oː ɔː
LOW		aː	

The Great English Vowel Shift affected the long vowels. It probably began with the diphthongization of [i] and [u]. The creation of the diphthongs [aj] and [aw] reduced the number of simple vowels from seven to five. The remaining vowels then shifted upwards in their articulation.

The vowel shifts are summarized below.

1. Long [i] became the diphthong [aj]
2. Long [u] became the diphthong [aw]
3. Long [e] became [i]
4. Long [ɛ] became [i]
5. Long [a] became [e]
6. Long [o] became [u]
7. Long [ɔ] became [o]

And as the vowels shifted, length was lost. After the Great English Vowel Shift, the long vowels now looked like:

	FRONT	CENTRAL	BACK
HIGH	i		u
MID	e	aj aw	o
LOW			

As is evident by comparing the above two charts, the overall effect of the vowel shift was a reduction in the number of vowels, thereby lessening the crowdedness of the phonological space.

Think ... Many of our vowel spellings reflect Middle English pronunciation. For example, the word 'goose' is spelled with 'oo' because this orthographic symbol represented [o:]. 'goose' continues to be spelled this way, even though as a result of the Great English Vowel Shift [o:] became [u], changing the pronunciation of 'goose' to [gus]. One reason for this mismatch between spelling and pronunciation is that spelling was standardized before the vowels had finished shifting!

Try this! For each of the Middle English words below, state the vowel change that would have occurred as a result of the Great Vowel Shift, and then give the spelling of corresponding Modern English word.

Middle English	Vowel Change	Modern English Word
[no:n]	_____	_____
[li:fə]	_____	_____
[swe:t]	_____	_____
[bɔ:st]	_____	_____
[gu:n]	_____	_____

MORPHOLOGICAL CHANGE

Morphological change affects the structure of words within a language. Morphological change involves either the addition or the loss of affixes. Recall from morphology that affixes are bound morphemes that attach to a base. Affixes provide grammatical information (inflection), or are used to create new words (derivation).

⇒ **The addition of affixes.** Some examples of how affixes can be added to a language are given in the box below.

TYPE	DEFINITION	EXAMPLE
Borrowing	Borrowed words frequently consist of a root and at least one affix. Eventually, these affixes may enter the language.	-ment and –able were borrowed from the French language.
Grammaticization	Grammaticization creates new grammatical forms from lexical forms. During grammaticization, (1) the semantic content of the lexical form is lost, and (2) lexical forms are reduced phonologically.	The Italian future suffix '-ō' developed from the Latin word 'habe'-ō' – have/hold/ grasp'.
Fusion	Fusion involves the development of an affix (either a prefix or a suffix) from two words that are frequently adjacent to each other. Over time, these words fuse together to form a base and a suffix, or a prefix and a base.	In Latin amāre and habeam fused together to become amābō.

⇒ **The loss of affixes.**   Affixes can also be lost.

Affixes sometimes just simply cease to be used. A good example of this is the Old English derivational suffix -bora, which is no longer found in Modern English.

Affixes can also be lost through sound change. Sound changes such as consonant deletion, vowel reduction, and vowel deletion caused the loss of Old English case endings.

The effect of adding or losing affixes.   The loss of affixes can result in a synthetic morphological system becoming analytic, while the addition of affixes can result in an analytic morphological system gradually becoming synthetic. An analytic language has very few inflectional affixes (e.g., Modern English). In contrast, a synthetic language has many inflectional affixes (e.g., Old English).

Try This! Folk Etymology is used to refer to the analysis of a word based on an incorrect historical division of that word into its morphemes. This is usually done without reference to the word's origins. Hence the use of the word 'folk'!

Identify the base and affix for each of the following words.

- yearling
- duckling
- gosling

- underling
- hireling
- nursling

Are the words in the second column as common as those in the first? Do they have the same meaning?

Historically, each of the above words consists of a base plus the affix –ing. This German affix has the meaning 'having the quality of'. What has happened to this affix in terms of its form? Why would such a reanalysis occur? What happened to the affix in terms of its meaning? What might have caused this shift?

What about the word *earthling*? How does this relate to the original German affix as well as the above words? What about the word *darling*?

QUICK REMINDER

Reanalysis and analogy can also affect the morphological structure of a language. Reanalysis adds new morphemes to a language, while analogy can change an existing morphological pattern.

SYNTACTIC CHANGE

Change can also affect the syntactic component of a language's grammar. Change often affects the word order patterns found in a language. It can also affect the transformations found within a language.

⇒ **Word Order.** Languages can change their basic word order pattern. One common change involves the change from an SOV (subject-object-verb) order to an SVO (subject-verb-object) order. This is a change that happened in the development of English. English descended from a Germanic language having an SOV order.

⇒ **Transformations.** Yes/no questions in English are formed using the Inversion transformation. In Old English, both main verbs and auxiliary verbs could be inverted. In Modern English, though, only auxiliary verbs can be inverted. Now, any sentence that does not contain an auxiliary must be made into a yes/no question using 'do'.

Try This! Below are some sentences from 16th century English along with their modern counterparts. Examine the sentences, and determine how negatives were formed. How does this differ from today's English?

1. A kinder gentleman treads not the Earth.
   A kinder gentleman doesn't tread the Earth.

2. Hate counsels not in such a quantity.
   Hate doesn't counsel in such a quantity.

3. Clamber not you up to the casement then.
   Don't climb up to the casement then.

CONNECTIONS

Changes can have far-reaching effects. A change that affects the phonology of a language can eventually affect the morphology, which in turn can affect the syntax of a language.

Consider an example (somewhat simplified) from the development of English.

⇒ Old English was a highly inflected language. Old English inflectional affixes included:

1.	Case:	Nominative, Accusative, Dative, Genitive
2.	Number:	Singular, Dual, Plural
3.	Person:	First, Second, Third
4.	Gender:	Masculine, Feminine, Neuter
5.	Tense:	Past, Present

Inflectional affixes were found on pronouns, nouns, articles, adjectives, verbs, etc. As in many inflected languages, Old English had a fairly free word order. Sentences with SVO, VSO, and SOV orders could all be found.

⇒ During Middle English, sound changes started happening in unstressed syllables. These sound changes included:

- m → n / _____#
- n → Ø / _____#
- a, o, u, i, e → ə / _____#

These three sound changes affected the inflectional system. Inflectional affixes in Old English were suffixes, and suffixes are typically not stressed. The following two examples illustrate the application of the above rules and their effect on the inflectional system.

Old English						**Middle English**
foxum	>	foxun	>	foxu	>	foxə
helpan	>	helpan	>	helpa	>	helpə

As a result of these sound changes, all the affixes became the same: 'ə'. Since it was now impossible to tell what information was contained in an affix, the Old English affixes were dropped.

⇒ But, speakers still needed to know what the subject of a sentence was, what the object of a sentence was, and what noun an adjective referred to. To get this information, speakers of English began to …

1. Rely on prepositions.
2. Rely on fixed word order (SVO).

So … sound changes can have a drastic effect on a language's development over time.

QUICK REMINDER!

Just like with phonological rules, sound changes also often require an order to their application. For example, the three rules presented in the last section require some ordering. [m] has to first change to [n] before it can be deleted. If this change does not occur first, then [n] would not delete and the affixes would not all become [ə]. Note that it doesn't matter when the vowel reduction rule applies!

LEXICAL CHANGE

Lexical change involves modifications to the lexicon. There are two main types of lexical change: addition and loss.

<u>Addition of Lexical Items</u>

New lexical items are typically added to a language's vocabulary in one of two ways.

⇒ **Word Formation.** Some of the morphological phenomena found in the Morphology chapter are frequently used to add new words to a language. These new words often fill a lexical gap resulting from technological innovations. Compounding and Derivation are probably the two most frequently used processes for this purpose. Acronyms, Backformation, Blends, Clipping, and Conversion can also be used to add new words to a language.

⇒ **Borrowing.** As languages come into contact, they often borrow words from each other. Borrowed words are often called loan words. There are three types of influences that languages can have on each other.

  • *Substratum Influence.* This type of influence results in the borrowing of place-names as well as names for unfamiliar objects or items. For example, English borrowed place-names such as Thames, London, and Dover from the Celtic language.

  • *Superstratum Influence.* This type of influence often results in borrowings related to all things official. For example, English borrowed many words from the French language during the Middle English period. French loan words are typically found in relation to government (e.g., government), religion (e.g., prayer), judiciary (e.g., judge), science (e.g., medicine), culture (e.g., sculpture), and warfare (e.g., army).

  • *Adstratum Influence.* Adstratum influence often results in the borrowing of common, everyday words. For example, English borrowed many Scandinavian words, including cake, egg, husband, score, window, and ugly.

Loss of Lexical Items

Words can also be lost from the vocabulary of a language. Loan words, non-loan words, compounds, and derived words can all be lost. The most common reason for the loss of a lexical item is some societal change that has rendered an object, and therefore its name, obsolete.

For example, English no longer uses the words flȳtme (a blood letting instrument) and eafor (tenant obligation to the king to convey goods), the compounds dimhus (prison) and aelfscīene (beautiful as a fairy), and the derived words manscipe (humanity) and heofonisc (heavenly).

SEMANTIC CHANGE

In addition to the addition and loss of lexical items, the meanings of existing words can also change over time. There are seven main types of semantic change.

TYPE	DEFINITION
Amelioration	The meaning of a word changes to become more positive or favourable. e.g., pretty 'tricky/sly/cunning' → 'attractive'
Broadening	The meaning of a word becomes more general or inclusive over time. e.g., aunt 'father's sister' → 'father or mother's sister'
Metaphor	A word with a concrete meaning takes on a more abstract meaning, without losing the original meaning. e.g., high → 'on drugs'
Narrowing	The meaning of a word becomes less general or inclusive over time. e.g., meat 'any type of food' → 'flesh of an animal'
Pejoration	The meaning of a word changes to become less positive or favourable. e.g., silly 'happy/prosperous' → 'foolish'
Shift	A word loses its former meaning and takes on a new, but related, meaning. e.g., bead 'prayer' → 'prayer bead'
Weakening	The meaning of a word weakens over time. e.g., soon 'immediately' → 'near future'

Practice! Practice! For each of the following words, identify which of the processes in the above table best captures the semantic change that has occurred.

Word	Earlier Meaning	Later Meaning	Semantic Change
1. aisle	passage between pews of a church	passage between rows of seats	_____
2. mischievous	disastrous	playfully annoying	_____
3. blue	a colour	being melancholy	_____
4. spill	shed blood	waste of liquid	_____
5. fond	foolish	affectionate	_____
6. butler	male servant in charge of the wine cellar	male servant in charge of a household	_____
7. passenger	traveller	one who travels by vehicle or vessel	_____
8. wretch	exile	unhappy person	_____
9. notorious	widely known	widely and unfavourably known	_____
10. chair	a seat	head of a university or college department	_____

COMPARATIVE RECONSTRUCTION

By comparing languages with each other, it can be determined if they are or are not genetically related. Genetically related languages are languages that have descended from a common ancestor. Using the comparative method, this ancestor can be reconstructed. This is typically done by comparing later forms to determine what the earlier form must have looked like. Although it is possible to reconstruct all aspects of a language's grammar, the focus here is on phonological reconstruction.

Some important terms ...

⇒ **Cognates** are phonetically and semantically similar words that have descended from a common source. Cognates are compared to reconstruct what this common source must have looked like.

⇒ A **proto-language** is a language that has been reconstructed using a comparative method. Written evidence of what this language actually looked like typically doesn't exist.

⇒ A proto-language consists of **proto-forms**. These are the individual reconstructed words of the proto-language. Proto-forms are usually indicated with a (*).

Some important strategies ...

⇒ **The Phonetic Plausibility Strategy** requires that any change posited to account for the differences between the proto-form (the ancestor) and the cognates must be phonetically plausible. That is, a sound change that has been found to occur in the course of language development must be able to account for these differences. For our purposes, the sound changes listed under the heading **sequential change**, as well as under **segmental** and **auditory change**, are all plausible.

⇒ **The Majority Rules Strategy** operates in the absence of a phonetically plausible sound change. This strategy states that when no phonetically plausible sound change can be determined, we may reconstruct the segment that occurs in the majority of the cognates. This strategy should only be used as a last resort.

An example ...

Reconstruct the proto-forms for the data below.

	Lang A	Lang B	Lang C
1.	hauda	hauta	hauta
2.	sav	ʃive	sav

⇒ **First.** Determine the number of sounds that need to be reconstructed. This is straightforward for (1) in that all the cognates have the same number of sounds: five. The situation is different in (2). In (2), two of the cognates contain three sounds, and one contains four. If four sounds are reconstructed, then deletion must have occurred in Lang A and C. If three sounds are reconstructed, then epenthesis must have occurred in Lang B. It is more plausible for deletion rather than epenthesis to occur at the end of words. (2), therefore, requires the reconstruction of four sounds.

⇒ **Second.** Look for any total correspondences. These are sounds which have not changed; they are the same for all the cognates. Reconstruct these sounds. The proto-forms after this step are: *hauʔa and *ʔʔvʔ.

⇒ **Third.** Examine alternations between the different languages and determine phonetic plausibility.

- (1) exhibits an alternation between [t] and [d]. Either [t] or [d] can be reconstructed in the proto-form. If [d] is reconstructed, then the change from the proto-form to the form in Lang B ([d] > [t]) does not correspond to a sound change. Therefore, this has a low phonetic plausibility. If [t] is reconstructed, then the change from the proto-form to Lang A and C ([t] > [d]) can be explained as an instance of weakening (a voiceless stop weakens to a voiced stop). This has a high phonetic plausibility. Reconstruct the change that has the highest phonetic plausibility. The proto-form, therefore, becomes *hauta.

- (2) exhibits three alternations. First, consider the alternation between [s] and [ʃ]. If [ʃ] is reconstructed, then the change [ʃ] > [s] in Lang A and C has low phonetic plausibility since it does not correspond to a sound change. If [s] is reconstructed, then the change [s] > [ʃ] in Lang B can be explained as palatalization. This has high phonetic plausibility and so [s] is reconstructed. Second, consider the presence or absence of a word-final vowel in the cognates. Recall from above that it is more plausible for a sound to delete then be epenthesized in this position. Therefore, [e] is reconstructed. Third, consider the vowel alternation between [a] and [i]. If [a] is reconstructed, then the change [a] > [i] occurs in Lang B, and if [i] is reconstructed, then the opposite change, [i] > [a], occurs in Lang A and C. Both do not correspond to a sound change and so have a low phonetic plausibility. This strategy, therefore, cannot be used to reconstruct this segment. The proto-form, after phonetic plausibility has been exhausted, is *sʔve.

⇒ **Fourth.** Any sounds for which no phonetically plausible sound change could be identified require using the Majority Rules Strategy. In (2), the alternation between [a] and [i] can not be accounted for using a sound change; therefore, [a] is reconstructed since it occurs in the majority of the cognates. The proto-form becomes *save. Notice that this proto-form does not correspond to any of the cognates. This is okay!

⇒ **Fifth.** Put together a summary of the sound changes that have occurred since the different languages split from the proto-language. Remember that the proto-form you have just reconstructed is older than the cognates from the descendent languages. Voicing and Apocope have occurred in the development of Lang A, while only Apocope occurred in the development of Lang C. Palatalization occurred in the development of Lang B.

REMINDER! REMINDER!

In order to do language reconstruction, you need to be able to identify phonetically plausible sound changes. And in order to do this, you need to know the different types of sequential, segmental, and auditory sound changes. Make sure you are very familiar with them!

Practice! Practice! Each data group below contains some cognate sets. Assume that all the cognates are in phonetic transcription and that all members of the cognate set have the same meaning. Reconstruct the proto-forms and list all the sound changes that have taken place in each language. Remember: for some languages there may be no sound changes, while for others there may be multiple sound changes.

While the data is from hypothetical or highly regularized data, it exemplifies processes found in actual languages.

GROUP ONE

	Lang A	Lang B	Proto-Form
1.	mũtə	muθo	* _____
2.	fumə	vumo	* _____
3.	pippon	bipona	* _____
4.	nõk	noga	* _____
5.	wus	juza	* _____
6.	fitə	vido	* _____

Summary of Sound Changes:

Lang A	
Lang B	

Remember … the reconstructed form does not have to be the same as any of the forms found in one of the descendent languages!

GROUP TWO

	Lang A	Lang B	Lang C	Lang D	Proto-Form
1.	puxa	buga	puka	puk	* _____
2.	nizudz	nizuz	mizu	nir	* _____

Summary of Sound Changes:

Lang A	
Lang B	
Lang C	
Lang D	

GROUP THREE

	Lang A	Lang B	Lang C	Lang D	Proto-Form
1.	pika	big	pik	biha	* _____
2.	wira	wil	wir	wira	* _____
3.	vida	bita	vit	viθa	* _____

Summary of Sound Changes:

Lang A	
Lang B	
Lang C	
Lang D	

GROUP FOUR

	Lang A	Lang B	Lang C	Proto-Form
1.	tuhu	tuu	tuhu	*_____
2.	nika	nika	nika	*_____
3.	kaza	kasa	kaʃa	*_____
4.	tuku	tuku	tuku	*_____
5.	juhu	juu	juhu	*_____
6.	pida	piθa	pita	*_____
7.	kadi	kaθi	kati	*_____
8.	kwazi	kwasi	kwaʃi	*_____

Summary of Sound Changes:

Lang A	
Lang B	
Lang C	

**REMINDER … Always look for a plausible sound change first.
Only use majority rules as a last resort.**

GROUP FIVE

	Lang A	Lang B	Lang C	Lang D	Proto-Form
1.	puxə	buga	pukka	puk	* _____
2.	lirə	liza	litsu	wis	* _____
3.	mani	mani	mãnni	mã	* _____
4.	wanə	jana	wãnna	wã	* _____
5.	kaxə	gaga	kakka	kak	* _____
6.	tupi	dubi	tubi	tup	* _____
7.	samu	samu	sãmmu	sã	* _____
8.	matu	madu	madu	mat	* _____

Summary of Sound Changes:

Lang A	
Lang B	
Lang C	
Lang D	

Now try this one!

Proto-Middle Indic   (Note: the data has been modified)

	Magadhi Prakrit	Pali Prakrit	Maharastri	Gloss
1.	[abala]	[apara]	[avara]	other
2.	[diba]	[dipa]	[diva]	lamp
3.	[hasta]	[hatta]	[hatta]	hand
4.	[loga]	[loka]	[loa]	world
5.	[nala]	[nara]	[nara]	man
6.	[nispʰala]	[nippʰala]	[nippʰala]	fruitless
7.	[paskʰaladi]	[pakkʰalati]	[pakkʰalai]	(he) stumbles
8.	[pidi]	[pita]	[pia]	father
9.	[puspa]	[puppa]	[puppa]	flower
10.	[ʃuska]	[sukka]	[sukka]	dry

Proto-forms:

1.	6.
2.	7.
3.	8.
4.	9.
5.	10.

Sound Changes:

Magadhi Prakrit	Pali	Maharastri Prakrit

RECONSTRUCTION AND INDO-EUROPEAN

In the late 18th century, Sir William Jones discovered that Sanskrit (the ancient language of India), Greek, Latin, and the Celtic and Germanic languages were all related. That is, words from these languages form cognate sets. It was eventually ascertained that the people who now inhabit Europe and Northern India at one time all spoke the same language. Using the comparative method, linguists have been able to reconstruct the proto-language from which languages such as English, German, Spanish, Welsh, and Russian descended. This ancestral language is called Proto-Indo-European (PIE).

The speakers of Proto-Indo-European probably lived somewhere in north or central Europe. They eventually began a series of migrations from their homeland. Within each migrating group, changes occurred to the proto-language until eventually each group spoke a different language.

In 1822, Jacob Grimm (of Grimm's Fairy Tales) noticed some regular sound correspondences between the Germanic languages and the non-Germanic Indo-European languages. The correspondences he noticed are listed below.

Non-Germanic Consonant	As in these Non-Germanic Words	Corresponding Germanic Consonant	As in these Germanic Cognates
[p]	**p**ater (Latin)	[f]	**f**ather (German – **V**ater)
[t]	**t**onare (Latin)	[θ]	**th**under
[k]	**c**anis (Latin)	[x] → [h]	**h**ound (German – **H**und)
[b]	kanna**b**is (Greek)	[p]	hem**p**
[d]	**d**uo (Latin)	[t]	**t**wo
[g]	a**g**er (Latin)	[k]	a**c**re
[bh]	**bh**rata (Sanskrit)	[b]	**b**rother (German – **B**ruder)
[dh]	vi**dh**ava (Sanskrit)	[d]	wi**d**ow
[gh]	**gh**ansas (Sanskrit)	[g]	**g**oose (German – **G**ans)

Grimm explained these correspondences using three sound changes. These sound changes are collectively known as Grimm's Law, which is an example of a sound shift.

(1) Voiceless stops became voiceless fricatives (i.e., weakening – frication)

PIE		Proto-Germanic (PIE)
[p]	>	[f]
[t]	>	[θ]
[k]	>	[x] → [h]

(2) Voiced stops became voiceless stops

PIE		PG
[b]	>	[p]
[d]	>	[t]
[g]	>	[k]

(3) Voiced aspirated stops became voiced unaspirated stops

PIE		PG
[bh]	>	[b]
[dh]	>	[d]
[gh]	>	[g]

The first of Grimm's rules involves the weakening of stops to fricatives. This, of course, is a phonetically plausible sound change. Sound changes that tend to occur across many languages are often referred to as natural. **Naturalness** is an important factor in reconstruction, since language change is regular and systematic. The result of this weakening process left Proto-Germanic without voiceless stops. Since it is rare for a language to completely lack voiceless stops, this gap was filled by devoicing the voiced stops. This change illustrates the role of **typological plausibility** in reconstruction: reconstruction should take into account the universal properties of language. The re-introduction of voiceless stops in turn created a lack of voiced stops. This new gap was filled by de-aspirating the voiced aspirated stops. This, of course, created yet another gap: a lack of voiced aspirated stops. This gap was not filled!

There are exceptions to Grimm's Law. Some systematic exceptions can be explained with a further rule, notably Verner's Law. Still other exceptions can be traced back to borrowings from Latin and French. Such borrowings did not undergo Grimm's Law or even Verner's Law, since these words entered the language long after the sound shift had occurred.

Using principles of reconstruction, along with naturalness and typological plausibility, scholars in the nineteenth century made major advances in classifying languages. Reconstruction is currently being used to determine the genetic relationships between hundreds of indigenous North American languages.

Try This! For each bolded sound in the reconstructed Proto-Indo-European (PIE) word, give the sound change that occurred as a result of Grimm's Law. Then give the Modern English equivalent of the proto-form.

	PIE WORD	GERMANIC SOUND (IN IPA)	ENGLISH WORD IN REGULAR SPELLING
1.	*g**el	_____	_____ool
2.	*le**b**	_____	li_____
3.	*grebh	_____	_____ra
4.	*ghreib	_____	_____ri_____
5.	*pulo	_____	_____oul
6.	*koimo	_____	_____ome
7.	*swad	_____	swee_____

REVIEW! REVIEW! Make sure you know:

- the causes of language change (5)
- the different types of sound change
- the difference between sequential, segmental, and auditory sound changes
- the difference between synthetic and analytic languages
- the different types of morphological change
- the different types of syntactic change
- the different types of lexical and semantic change
- how change spreads through a language and its population
- how to reconstruct proto-forms and identify sound changes
- the three sound changes making up Grimm's Law
- the role of naturalness in language change
- the relationship between change and typology

QUESTIONS? PROBLEMS? DIFFICULTIES?

_____

_____

_____

_____

_____

_____

_____

_____

_____

_____

_____

NOTES

NOTES

NOTES

NOTES

NOTES

NOTES